LEARNING TO WRITE/WRITING TO LEARN

JOHN S. MAYHER
New York University

NANCY B. LESTER
The Write Company

GORDON M. PRADL
New York University

BOYNTON/COOK PUBLISHERS
HEINEMANN
PORTSMOUTH, NH

5

Boynton/Cook Publishers
A Division of
Heinemann Educational Books, Inc.
70 Court Street, Portsmouth, NH 03801
Offices and agents throughout the world

Library of Congress Cataloging in Publication Data

Mayher, John Sawyer.
Learning to write/writing to learn.
1. English language—Composition and exercises—Study and teaching. 2. Language arts. 3. Study, Method of.
I. Lester, Nancy, 1939- II. Pradl, Gordon M. III. Title.
PE1404.M38 1983 418' 007 83-15154
ISBN 0-86709-073-1

Printed in the United States of America
89 90 91 92 93 9 8 7 6 5

Acknowledgments

This book had its beginnings with the New York University-CBS Sunrise Semester Course of the same title, which was broadcast during the Spring of 1980. John was the anchorman for the course, and Nancy and Gordon assisted throughout on its planning and execution. The course was greatly strengthened by the appearance of a number of nationally and internationally prominent teachers/scholars concerned with the teaching of writing. Some of their contributions have been included in this version, and we're grateful to all of them for their willingness to share their time and expertise with us and the course's audience.

The text itself also reflects the feedback and contributions of the teachers/students who participated in the course and who have worked with us since in in-service workshops in Arizona and in the New York metropolitan area. If we've been successful in saying things that teachers need to hear in ways that will be useful to their teaching, it's largely the result of the help we've received from those practicing teachers who are struggling to improve the way they teach writing. Thus, hearty thanks to: Nina Woolf, Harold Vine, Bonnie Thompson, Karen Shawn, Cindy Rudrud, John Rouse, Louise Rosenblatt, Sondra Perl, Bob Parker, Cynthia Onore, Lee Odell, Bucky Nickau, Cheryl Miceli, Philip Lopate, Cy Knoblauch, Paula Johnson, Lynn Jett, Lisa Ann Jarvi, Diane Hilser, Mary K. Healy, Fred Grossberg, Karen Greenberg, Barbara Gray, Margaret Grant, Laurel Fritz, Linda Flower, Janet Emig, Molly Carmody, Elaine Caret, Joe Cammarano, Lucy Calkins, Diane Burkhardt, Lillian Buie, Becky Brown, Rita Brause, Dale Boyd, Martha Bell, and Kathrine Becker.

One person was omitted from the above list because he deserves special mention. Jimmy Britton, to whom this book is dedicated, was gracious enough to appear as a guest on three of the TV shows, and his pervasive intellectual and personal influence is manifest throughout the text. We have deliberately chosen not to quote his taxonomies of writing functions extensively because we intend the book to be introductory. But his conversation and writing have consistently influenced and inspired our work.

This book attempts, in part, to place in an American context many of the ideas about the teaching of writing which were first developed in England. The British-American connection, originated at the Dartmouth Conference in 1966, was cemented by the collaboration of British and American English educators at the New York University Summer Abroad Program at the University of York begun by Gordon and John in 1975 with the able assitance of Geoffrey Summerfield.

In *Learning to Write/Writing to Learn* we continually emphasize the importance of a learning community. We have been fortunate enough to participate in such a community at New York University. Our colleagues, both students and faculty, have demonstrated clearly that teaching-learning is a reciprocal compound noun. Because during our combined years at NYU we have learned from too many students to mention them all, we would just like to say a collective thank you to all of them. We would, however, like to recognize our teaching colleagues: Sue Livingston, Mitchell Leaska, Terry Morgan, Angela Jaggar, Harvey Nadler, Chris Nystrom, Mirian Eisenstein, Neil Postman, Bea Cullinan, Bob Berlin, Lenore Ringler, Roger Cayer, Carl Schmidt, Lil Brannon, Trika Smith-Burke, Joy Boyum, Marilyn Sobelman, Harold Vine, and Bob Willis.

Our own intellectual collaboration has been both long and fruitful, and it made the production of this text an almost entirely joyous experience. John and Gordon first met in a doctoral seminar at Harvard in the fall of 1967, and they've been trying to help each other overcome writer's block ever since. Nancy joined the team in the mid-seventies and provided the energy without which there would be no book. Even at three in the morning, after a long session of deleting precious words from the manuscript, we were still speaking to each other. Finally, we'd like to include in our thanks Peter Stillman of Boynton/Cook for his commitment to cutting the cull from those passages we passed over in the early morning sessions and Mary Ann Pradl for her patience and fortitude.

Three other notes should be made about the text itself. Throughout you will find comments on the issues discussed in each chapter. These were excerpted from the remarks contributed by our guests on the Sunrise Semester program. Second, you will find *Writing to Learn* activities at the end of each chapter. We have already used them successfully with the students in our our Sunrise Semester course, and hope they will engage you in the learning processes of the book. And third, there is no satisfactory solution for the absence of a neutral gender pronoun in English. We have, therefore, chosen to alternate the use of *she* and *he* in each chapter, beginning with *she* in Chapter 1.

Contents

1

Introduction

We've called this book *Learning to Write/Writing to Learn* for two reasons: First, research indicates that the only way one learns to write is by writing. While other ways of using language, most particularly reading, can contribute to the growth of writing ability, there's no substitute for extensive experience with writing itself. Thus, one sense of "writing to learn" means that through writing one is learning to write; the second sense of "writing to learn" is that writing can be a means for learning. When we write a report of what we observe in a science laboratory or when we try to synthesize material garnered from multiple sources for a social studies paper, the actual process of doing such writing can be an integral part of learning the content of these disciplines. Both of these views of writing depend upon a nontraditional view of learning: it's not a process of ingesting and regurgitating the teacher's information, or acquiring and developing skills, but a personally engaging transaction through which the learner makes her own connections and builds her own meaning.

We have written this book for teachers of all grade levels, K-14, and all disciplines. Although English and language arts teachers have traditionally been the only teachers of writing, using writing as a means of learning is hardly their exclusive province. One of the principal problems that students and teachers face in learning a subject has been the assumption that writing is something reserved exclusively for English classes.

In this book the term *writing* will be broadly defined as *language choice on paper. Choice* is important because it emphasizes the selection process, which is crucial to writing, and because it enables us to say that copying is *not* writing. Further, it seems clear that regurgitative exercises such as filling in the blanks and answering recall questions only barely fall within our definition. *Language* is central to our definition because, as will be seen throughout the book, we stress the linguistic basis for learning to write. *On paper* seems obvious at first, but it's important to emphasize that language on paper is malleable, even erasable, before it becomes permanent. While the apparent permanence of writing can be scary to inexperienced writers, they have to learn that although spoken language choices can't be recalled or reshaped, their written choices are changeable until they declare, "I'm finished." Recognizing this leads to a sense of confidence and, above all, to a sense of control.

This broad definition of writing makes its relationship to learning in all content areas more apparent. Since writing in this sense includes list making, note taking, observational sketching, and journal writing, as well as more formal types of writing, it's easy to see that there's plenty of room for the kind of tentative exploring on paper, of trial and error, which is the hallmark of learning. Underlying this definition is a view of learning as an active process in which the learner is trying to make sense of new information by connecting it with what she already knows. The process of writing demands that these connections be made explicit and potentially public. Doing so reveals to both teacher and learner what has been learned and what still must be learned. Keeping a "learning log," for instance, provides a valuable format for private student-teacher dialogue on what's working well and what's troubling the student. Frequently, the student's framing a question or diagnosing her own learning problem can lead to its solution.

Recording, reporting, classifying, and generalizing as well as interpreting, reflecting, imagining, and speculating—all include uses of writing. We will return to the role that each of these processes can play in learning, but consider now that none of them involves merely transcribing pre-existent knowledge; all require an active process of discovery.

Another important aspect of writing to learn is writing to learn about oneself. Diary entries, autobiographical fragments, responses to stories, statements of belief or philosophy—each helps the writer clarify who she is. By using language to explore feelings and personal history, the writer comes to understand herself better. Such writing might lead to artistic creation in the form of stories, poems, or plays, or it might serve simply as self-discovery.

And, of course, by engaging in these types of writing one is constantly learning to write. Teachers have too often viewed writing as a skill that can be learned independently of any actual need to write. This has led to writing instruction dominated by workbook exercises or dummy runs.

Purpose and Audience

Real writing involves a purpose and an audience. The purpose, even if it's writing to fulfill an assignment, must finally be the writer's. Good writers learn to make even the most boring assignment their own. They learn that during the act of writing they will discover what they want to say. Until a writer has discovered this, neither she nor anyone else can begin to evaluate whether she has said it adequately.

Helping students find or develop a genuine purpose in school writing is one of the most challenging aspects of writing instruction. It's all too easy for teachers to assume that *their* purposes for student writing are the same as students', although this is rarely the case, or to fall back on grades and other extrinsic motivations to disguise the fact that the writing itself is purposeless. Having a real audience can help, but the essential ingredient in finding purpose is the writer's conviction that she has something to say. Students must come to recognize that they know a great deal and have experiences worth sharing with others. Unless a writer gets sufficiently involved in developing her own ideas and beliefs, the writing will not be worth reading no matter how mechanically correct it is.

Just as writing cannot be for dummy purposes, neither can it be for a dummy audience. Writing which serves a real purpose, whether it be lists, letters, notes, memos, or more extensive reports, always has a real audience. But most school writing has only the teacher as its audience. Student writers perceive teachers, on the one hand, as having all the answers and, on the other, as being more concerned with conventions than ideas. Ironically, teachers are also not ideal audiences for student writing because they are often too good. That is, they read well, work hard at trying to make sense of the most incoherent prose, and tend to be too kind to students in their responses.

Furthermore, teachers are required to evaluate, and this function frequently supersedes all other feedback from teachers to students about their writing. The process of writing to the teacher as evaluator often becomes one of trying to figure out what needs to be done in order to get a good grade. Student writers often understand writing to be mastery of a series of forms, with little concern for meaning, or as an appropriate regurgitation of information.

In short, any comparison between real world writing and school writing leads us to two conclusions. First, teachers should not be the sole audience for student writing. Second, all student writing should have student-determined purposes even when based on a teacher's assignment.

Writing as a Linguistic Process

Like speaking, reading, and listening, writing draws on the resources of that most human of attributes—our language system. The infinite potential for expression contained in each human language, is, in principle, available to even the most inexperienced writer. Another area for exploration is the connections among the various modes of language use. Because learning to write is not as automatic as learning to speak, children normally learn to write in school. One of the hypotheses that underlies our view of learning to write, however, is that given the right contexts it can be nearly as natural a process as learning to talk. Just as young children learn to speak and understand because they live within a speech community that provides them with a purpose and audience for their talk, so an environment which provides a purpose and audience for writing is essential for the development of writing ability.

There are linguistic structures, both syntactic and semantic, more commonly used in writing than speech. This doesn't require, however, that they be "taught"; they are acquired implictly through extensive reading and actual writing. By reading and writing, students can learn the special properties, demands and constraints of the written system. Standard written English can be thought of as a unique variety of English which, although no one actually speaks it, has distinct properties that need mastering if one hopes to be able to read and write well.

Speakers of all varieties of English have at their command the potential to create and understand an infinite range of sentences. Individual speakers differ from one another—in regional and social dialects, in individual vocabularies, and in differing capacities to use the resources of their linguistic system. Learning to write can be a way of extending linguistic resources. Both reading and writing can have a major impact on increasing vocabulary and enriching the range of syntactic and semantic complexity which each learner can use.

The best way to understand and encourage the interaction between the child's growing linguistic system and her emerging ability to write is to see the latter as a developmental process, which first emphasizes *fluency,* then *clarity,* and finally *correctness.* In stressing *fluency,* the goal is to build a sense of comfort, confidence, and control in the growing writer. Young writers must feel that they have ideas and a language system in their heads and that they can combine these to fill up blank sheets of paper. Only when words fill the page can we emphasize *clarity*: does the writing make sense to others? The final concern is whether or not the text conforms to the conventions of standard written English and is, therefore, correct. These three dimensions, of course, continually overlap; even the youngest writers must engage in some struggles for clarity and correctness, and even the most experienced writer has frequent problems with fluency—particularly when writing on a new topic or in a new genre.

As broad emphases, however, it seems clear that encouraging a young writer's fluency will develop her ability to determine her own purposes for writing so that then she can turn her primary emphasis to clarity, which relates directly to a desire to be understood by some audience. Our reasons for focusing last on correctness are that there's little point in having a "correct" paper without clear content and that a crippled or fearful writer is generally one who worries constantly about making mistakes. It's safe to say that there are millions of Americans for whom writing is a crippling burden, one to be avoided whenever possible, and that most of them got that way through a correctness-first, clarity-second, and fluency-sometimes-later-if-at-all approach.

The Composing Process

Another source of the ideas that underlie our approach to writing instruction has been the study of the way people actually compose. This research effort, pioneered by Janet Emig (1969) and extended by Donald Graves (1975), Linda Flower (1978), Sondra Perl (1979), and many others, has shown an interesting mixture of consistency and idiosyncracy in the ways writers of varying age and ability compose.

Although there's some disagreement as to exactly how many components are involved and how they interrelate, the writing of writers of all ages and abilities is essentially characterized by: *percolating, drafting, revising, editing,* and *publishing.*

Percolating involves everything that happens to the writer apart from the actual setting of marks on paper. It can include such informal but essential activities as thinking, talking, or reading about what one is writing, and some practical activities such as dramatics, role-playing and (particularly with young children) drawing. Percolating involves incubating, comtemplating, or rehearsing the experiences and ideas to be expressed in writing. Through percolating, the writer begins to discover what she wants to say.

It's necessary to distinguish what we have called "percolating" from what others, locked into linear "stage" notions of the composing process, have called "prewriting." First, percolating as opposed to prewriting happens throughout the writing process. Rereading what one has written is, for instance, a percolating activity. So is discovering that one doesn't know enough yet, which may lead to reading or talking to find out more. Second, as James Britton once remarked, "all of life is a prewriting activity." He emphasizes this both to discourage dummy run prewriting exercises and to stress the importance of what he calls "shaping at the point of utterance"—that the writer makes previously unrealized meanings at the precise moment that words are being written on paper.

Shaping at the point of utterance ties writing firmly to talking, and Britton emphasizes our capacity to say what we want to say at the moment of need without conscious planning. This capacity functions completely out of awareness because, he emphasizes, we're concerned with what we're saying, not with how we're saying it.

One of the most important aspects of *drafting* is the recognition that it's just that: one of the great advantages of writing over talking is that our initial expression can and often must be recast. One major finding of composing-process research has been to emphasize the importance of revision. Drafting and *revising,* then, are really two sides of the same coin, and teachers must learn to help students view their first expressions tentatively and become both willing and able to improve them through revision. One can revise entirely on the basis of one's own reading of the work, but a writer who intends to communicate to an audience will often profit from getting feedback on a draft from one or more members of that potential audience. For student writers particularly, empathetic and constructive feedback may be the most important basis for revising.

Feedback is particularly important for inexperienced writers who tend to assume that because the idea they were trying to express was clear to them, the text they've produced must necessarily be clear to a reader. This rather natural egocentricity frequently results in our reading our texts in such a way that we're actually "reading" our thought processes rather than the words. We may fill in omitted words, expand undeveloped thoughts, and mentally punctuate unpunctuated passages without noticing that we're doing so. Successful *editing* means learning to read the text that's actually there as though we'd never seen it before.

Editing should not begin too early since it's perfectly natural for drafts to be full of errors and omissions. Inexperienced writers frequently believe that their texts have to be right the first time. This causes them to get so concerned with questions of form that they never get much said. Correct form is important, of course; readers have very little patience for misspellings or grammatical errors, and many punctuation problems can actually cause confusion; but separating editing from the rest of the composing process can reduce anxiety and promote risk-taking.

Editing will be most natural and most important when the text is to be *published*. By *publishing* we mean any public presentation, which can range from posting the paper on the class bulletin board to actually sending the letter, or to putting out a class newspaper or school magazine. Any publishing activity helps broaden the audience for students' work and provides motivation for writing as well. Effective writing teachers find many ways to publish student work and by doing so help bridge the gap between real world writing, where publication of some sort is always the goal, and school writing, where it almost never has been except for the gifted few.

The drafting, revising, and editing aspects of the composing process are closely tied to our developmental emphasis on fluency, clarity, and correctness. Percolating and drafting are most closely associated with fluency in that they involve getting words on paper. Revising is directly related to clarity since audience feedback about whether or not the writing is clear can be crucial to revision. Finally, editing and publishing can be directly connected with correctness, and the important thing about both is that they not be approached too early.

Another important aspect of this process emerges from the study of how we make meaning when we read. Investigations of readers' responses to texts have revealed that meaning is made through a transaction between the words on the page and the reader who's making sense of them. A reader's experience, knowledge, personality, linguistic ability, and a host of other factors can influence her interpretation of the text. While this is well understood in the study of literature, its implications for the teaching of writing have not been developed.

The meaning of every text is what the reader makes of it. The writer is responsible for making her text as accessible as possible, thereby improving the chances that her intended meaning will be the one constructed by the reader. This relationship between the inner sphere of intention and the outer sphere of interpretation and the possible difference between the two provides a connection between our interactive view of the composing process and the idea that writing has a purpose and is directed to an audience.

Responding and Evaluating

The value of feedback from a reader as an aid to a writer's matching her text with her intentions cannot be overemphasized. Although fellow students and a variety of others can be enlisted, the most important source of feedback for school writing will undoubtedly continue to be the teacher. Therefore, teachers need to become better responders to student writing, which involves being clear about those response strategies that seem helpful and those that may be harmful.

The most helpful kind of feedback for any piece of writing must be given before the writer considers it to be finished. Although such responses may imply a judgment, they must not be judgmental. What the writer most needs to know is what sense the reader has made of what she's written. Even suggestions for improvement, however apt they may be, must take second place to an accurate reflection of what the reader understood the writer to be saying.

This means that explicit judgments of evaluation should be deferred as long as possible. Although most teachers will eventually have to evaluate student writing, they should always do it in a way that will facilitate learning. The issue of assessment is one of the most complex and highly charged aspects of teaching writing. Every English teacher has experienced that sinking feeling when piles of student papers threaten to swamp them. While we promise no magical solutions, we'll suggest some paths out of this quagmire in Chapter 7.

Growing Learners in the Classroom

Perhaps our most important goal in this book is to help teachers run writer- and learner-centered classrooms. We believe in such a setting because it works to help students learn to write and to recognize the values of writing as a tool for their own learning and as a way of interacting with others, to get them involved in their own destiny as writer-learners, and to create a classroom that's energy-giving rather than energy-draining.

Nothing we can *say* to students will convince them that writing will be of value to their present and future lives. Exercises and dummy run compositions will only confirm them in their belief that writing is some kind of painful rite of passage into the adult world. The only alternative is to make writing real. For writing to matter, there have to be real ideas being discovered, developed, shaped, and shared. For learning to matter, it must be connected to the present life of the learner as well as to the future.

Achieving such a classroom climate and helping students take control of their own learning won't be easy. Taking responsiblity for one's own learning isn't the way it's 'spozed to be for either student or school, especially when our institutitions seem to be moving in the direction of even more exercises, more drills. For many students the pervasive unreality of school seems exactly right because it permits them to devote their energy to their life outside of school and merely coast from 8:30 to 2:30. We're not overly optimistic that our message can do much to change things, but as teachers we must keep trying. For as we write in the shadow of 1984, it seems clear that the need for writer-learners has never been greater.

One final suggestion: in order to achieve a classroom where writers are writing and learners are learning, the teacher must be personally involved as a writer-learner. Teachers, like most adults, suffer badly from fears about their own writing. Ironically, English teachers often suffer the worst cases of correctness freeze-up. Change will only come to the classroom as the teacher becomes a fellow learner, sharing drafts, admitting error, asking for help.

While it may be true that teachers helping students learn to write don't have to be effective writers themselves, it's certainly true that teachers who write extensively and enjoy writing will be more comfortable and successful teaching writing. Teachers should at least write some of the assignments they give their students, both to understand what they've actually demanded and to be able to develop appropriate evaluation criteria. Teachers should also find forms of writing which are meaningful to them and develop some ways for getting feedback.

Some of the suggestions, questions, and activities that follow each chapter are designed to provide experiences that will enact our basic position of the value of using writing to learn. The lesson we teach is really the lesson we model for our students. We need not always be expert practitioners of everything we teach—we can't know or do it all flawlessly—but we can be the best learners we know how to be.

That, after all, is what we're teaching: not grammar or mathematics or history or cooking, but how to learn so that each time we try something it works a little better. To help our students grow as learners is our reason for teaching.

WRITING TO LEARN

1. People write for a variety of reasons and in a variety of settings, much wider than the traditional classroom essay would suggest. To become more aware of the range of writing possibilities in both your professional and personal lives, try remembering, then listing, all the occasions when you have actually written something (even just a few words) during the last several weeks.

Did you find yourself writing a longer list than you expected?

2. Now brainstorm a list that goes beyond your current writing habits. Include all those occasions when you might use or generate written language but at present don't do so. (You can also include things you'd like to do—if you had the time and the ability.) Now, what reason would there be for writing on each of these occasions? In the week ahead, try writing for some new purpose that you have identified in your hypothetical list.
3. Brainstorm a list containing all the many occasions and reasons your students might use writing, both inside and outside the classroom. How might this list change depending on the age of the student and the subject being studied? How much of this writing is student-generated? Teacher-generated? How frequently do students actually write in your classroom? Can you begin to speculate on how important a function writing plays in the teaching-learning strategies of your curriculum? How committed are other teachers and administrators to encouraging active writing in your school?
4. Take the three lists you've brainstormed and indicate both the *purpose* and *audience* for each item. How many different purposes are served? How many audiences are addressed? Do you see any contrasting patterns depending on whether or not the writing is done inside or outside of the classroom or school context?
5. We've begun here to make our case for the value of writing across the curriculum or writing to learn. Write a personal response which defines your position on writing to learn. What are your concerns or questions? The audience for your writing here is primarily yourself, but it might be interesting to do this again when you've finished the book and see how (or if) you've changed your mind.
6. Despite our good intentions to the contrary, most of the occasions for student writing end up having the teacher as primary audience. What other audiences might students realistically address in the context of your classroom? What might you do to encourage communication with these other audiences in your teaching? How do you think having a wider range of audiences will affect the writing of your students?
7. Find an audience or audiences for your own writing which you can use for the writing that will be suggested in subsequent chapters in this book. To cement your commitment, tell your audience that they can be expecting some writing from you in the near future, and that you'll be looking forward to responses to this writing.

2

Constructing Our World Through Writing

You, us, we're all incorrigible storytellers. "Well, I remember once when . . . " "Did you hear about . . . " "So let me tell you what happened . . . " As events swirl about us, the stories we tell and imagine are the means by which we make sense of our lives. Until we enforce some narrative structure to capture and interpret random events, the chronology of our lives appears like the unsegmented sound stream of a foreign language or strange dialect as it speeds by our untrained ears.

Our stories give us some coherent sense of a journey within time's flow, and so our own stories never appear arbitrary to us. We think we're merely recounting what is out there, obvious for anyone who would take the time to see. But just as we apply a set of linguistic conventions to divide up sound streams into words, sentences, and longer structural units, so we're socialized within our culture to filter events into what become reasonably predictable patterns.

A creative tension exists between what appears to be actually there before our eyes as a unique idiosyncratic story and what is simply a representative type of a story, one that highlights themes and concerns defined by our primary social groups. Conception, in other words, makes perception possible. With our mind focusing on completing a given task from getting asked to the Senior Prom to winning the Thanksgiving Day game, we accordingly shape what we see and, consequently, tell about. Still our story scripts aren't always so inevitably predetermined. New invention, from time to time, reverses the direction of this conception/perception equation. An unexpected success or failure of sufficient magnitude might jar us loose from an otherwise set pattern and propel us in a different direction. A new means of livelihood or place to live or even marriage partner will have a profound impact on the stories we tell.

In telling our stories we rely on the shaping questions that comprise the varied responses of our audiences. Was the car really going that fast? How many days do you have to stay after school? She did *what*? Well, what are you going to try next? Such responses constrain our leaps of imagination, forcing us to conform to the boundaries of reality that our audience demands. These demands establish the criteria we apply to our own emerging sense of self. Do our perceptions square with the image of what we would like to be? Are we too shy, too foolish, too vulnerable? Are we brave enough, wise enough? Is life passing us by or do we anticipate new adventures and successes? Are we depending upon our own talents and skills or waiting for luck and the plots of others to dictate results? Under scrutiny, our stories both conceal and reveal our innermost needs and desires.

JOHN ROUSE: Story is everything. All writing of whatever kind begins with narrative. In the first story, the primal story from which all others come, is your own story—your own personal history; the tale you'd tell about yourself if you chose. Whatever you write, no matter how abstract or impersonal it might be, is always telling some part of your own story. It's impossible to put pen to paper without revealing something about yourself.

There are three basic developmental aspects to storytelling. The first are the details out of which we construct a piece of writing or message. The second are feelings about these events and our commitment to them as an individual. To us that is what is real. The story we can tell—that's reality we know. The third stage is the summing up, the finding out of themes and patterns in our lives.

At the first stage, as a very young child, you have no sense of history. At the next stage you have a sense of the past and the present. In the final stage there's a summary and conclusion as well as a looking forward to the future in an attempt to construct events that will satisfy your needs and expectations.

The other side of constraint is possibility. Telling it can indeed make it so. Thus with many of our stories, we rehearse roles and exercise powers that prepare us for the future. In play young children tell stories that project how it will be when they grow older and must assume adult roles. They tell stories about making a career, establishing relationships, having families of their own. When a crucial event looms in the future, we practice the faculties we'll need for success by imagining scenarios that might describe this event, be it marriage, changing our job, beginning a new school year, purchasing a home, or preparing for a death in our family. Certain "what ifs" fit better than others, and so on the strength of these stories, we ride into a future that we're continually constructing for ourselves. Such analysis isn't intended to paralyze us with self-consciousness; rather, we need to recognize the pervasive nature of narrative in keeping both our private and public lives together.

The child's primary initiation into the speech community involves listening to and making up stories. Were our schools to follow the lead of the child's beginning formative environment, they would greatly increase the opportunities for telling stories and then for recording them in writing. What more natural transition into writing is there for the child in terms of "What should I write about?" than the need to get down in permanent form the latest narrative that has impressed itself upon his mind? Relating the birth of kittens, describing the fight on the playground, inventing a monster from outer space, each will serve in its own way. Bombarded by the fictions of the media, children risk losing their imaginative capacities unless they're encouraged to invent stories. Many of these stories will be derivative of modern culture, owing their origins to anything from Batman to Barney Miller, but at least the primary human power to create narrative is exercised.

JOHN MAYHER: What sort of purposes do children bring to writing?

JAMES BRITTON: There is no doubt that one of the intentions they bring with them to school is that of making sense of experience as it comes to them. As an instrument for making sense of experience, writing can help them fulfill that deep-seated intention. If we're right in what we're saying—that you shape experience in talking or writing about it—then to find shape in the world we live in is a major need, a major intention.

JOHN MAYHER: And yet schools as they are presently organized don't seem to recognize that the personal experiences of students are legitimate concerns in the classroom.

JAMES BRITTON: I agree; this represents a major split in teaching. Some teachers want to make schools a very specialized learning environment, making in-school learning very unlike out-of-school learning. I want to reverse that. I feel that the more in-school learning can become a part of a total learning pattern which equally covers in-school and out-of-school learning, the more effective the in-school learning is going to be.

JOHN MAYHER: But don't many teachers feel that personal writing takes valuable time away from academic writing?

JAMES BRITTON: To outlaw personal writing is to outlaw a very important way of relating even the most academic syllabus in the long run to the life of the child himself and the learning process

> the child has. If you can tap that kind of intention—the intention to make sense of experience—and if you can set up an environment where writing at the point of utterance is valued, then I think we're on to the kind of teaching and learning in schools that may look very different from an academic curriculum and much more like a modeling process.

Our stories point like dreams to certain themes or concerns in our lives, containing either explicitly or implicitly some moral tag which both sums up where we've been and points us in the "right" direction. Were our stories to have no point, audiences would soon lose interest. So in a sense the receiver of a story is always judging how well the storyteller answers a question, explains a mystery, relates to some larger underlying proposition. The specific answer doesn't matter, but some answer should be forthcoming. Otherwise the narrative circuit goes uncompleted, and our complementary need for interpretation and abstract summary remains frustrated.

When we look at stories in relation to their meanings we discover that narrative provides the essential foundation of exposition—that expository prose is merely a way of elaborating in more abstract form the truths that have been culled from a series of related or recurring stories. In expository form chronology is transformed into a hierarchical structure. Compare, for instance, a story that reveals how we lose our integrity by blindly conforming to the dictates of others vs. an essay on the danger of conformity in American society. In the first case, the "message" is rooted in the particulars of individual lives as we move from the concrete story to the generalization. The essay arises out of the author's experiences and subsequent reflections on conformity, but its structure is organized in the opposite direction, from abstraction to fact or incident. In either case, it's the story that is felt first. It becomes the jumping-off point, the way in. It provides the intentional urge that generates language structures which upon refinement may be satisfactory in themselves, or which may serve as the beginning for reasoned arguments and statements of value and belief that eventually may be expressed in essays.

Teachers Tell Stories

When as part of the assignments for *Sunrise Semester* we asked teachers to write down some of their own stories, the response was overwhelming. Many of their unrehearsed narratives spoke of incidents in which their identity or character was shaped through interaction with others. One woman recounts a crush she had had on one of her high school English teachers. This writer's subsequent commentary reveals the range of emotions that our stories help us capture, order and evaluate:

> Sophomore year. Still wet behind the ears. But not wetter than Mr. Tortello, the new English teacher in school. He decided to teach after finally giving up the idea of becoming a priest. This was his first teaching job.
>
> I liked the shakiness in his voice when he read from "Sohrab and Rustum" and the casual way he retold the story as if he were reading a newspaper account for a college radio station. He wasn't Billy Graham, however, and his gentle voice didn't exactly inspire, let alone keep everyone awake. But I watched his lips move and saw the sparkle in his eyes when he digested a line of verse that pleased him. He had a priestly glow on his forehead; he was a man of peace. That brow only wrinkled a deep wrinkle when kids were talking to each other while he read aloud. Sometimes he threw a piece of white chalk at the intruder in mock anger as the rude student ducked behind his poetry book.
>
> Then the teacher would smile showing his white protruding teeth. I licked the opaque plastic brace retainer under my front teeth and wondered why he never fixed those buck teeth. But they were kind of cute and innocent like their tall, skinny, boyish owner.
>
> Sometimes when he forgot which homework assignment he had given, I was always there to remind him, and when he asked a question about Sohrab or Rustum and the class drew a blank, I was there waving my hand with the wanted answer.
>
> Not that I was a goody-goody mind you. I was the type of student who would tell a joke that would break up the whole class for several minutes, but I would raise my hand and be called on before I came out with a pun aptly related to the text we were studying. How could a teacher reprimand you if you raised your hand politely first. Ah, the psychology of it was quite inspired!
>
> In any event, Mr. Tortello appreciated that I was his savior, and I didn't find it a big sacrifice because I had already fallen madly in love with him. Sometimes on snowy days he'd drive me home from school in his old black Packard with a running board on the side. I would have stayed in the seat next to the driver's seat until July. My heart beat rapidly and I talked just as rapidly to cover up for my nervousness.
>
> "I liked the way you read from *The Rime of the Ancient Mariner* today. 'Water, water everywhere, and not a drop to drink!' What an image. I shall never forget that line." "Did I really read it well? Thanks," he answered.
>
> Did you know how I adored you? I suppose so, but you brushed me off in a business-like fashion. You let me out of the car as if you were dismissing me.
>
> But you smiled so happily when I walked into class each day. Was it

my imagination that you were especially glad to see me the day after I was absent? Didn't you seem a bit fidgety when I moved a little closer to you in the old Packard whose heater never worked?

* * *

I met you years later at a high school production. My babysitter (I was now married with my own child) was in the play. You were English Department Chairperson now. You gave me a warm hello. My kiss grazed your cheek. "Let me introduce you to my wife," you said. She was a skinny, prim and proper dandelion; one strong wind would have done her in. She was like a nun with a white cotton blouse up to her chin. You smiled at me and at her with your buck teeth. You'd never had your teeth fixed. Did you marry her because you'd given up the priesthood so you felt that God wouldn't understand your marrying a Raquel Welch-type? Was she your penance? Does your heart beat wildly as you sit next to her in the station wagon with your eight kids in the back seat?

Commentary

This incident is important to me because it clearly showed me that people do not change. Mr. T. was the same physically (buck teeth) and mentally (he only let my kiss graze his cheek upon meeting him years later). And my feelings toward him hadn't changed much either. No, I was not madly in love with him; the schoolgirl crush was long over. But upon meeting him after so many years I still tried to put him on a pedestal. I walked over to him with admiration in my eyes wanting to be sixteen again. And he pushed me away with the turn of the cheek and business-like words, "Let me introduce you to my wife."

Oh, if only he had let me open the floodgates. What a waterfall of passion we could have created together. Then the words he had read so many years ago resounded in my ears, this time holding a new meaning: "Water, water everywhere and not a drop to drink."

This commentary illustrates the movement from narrative to exposition. Indeed, what is exposition if not some extended commentary on a story? And here right in front of us is a proposition worth examining: "People do not change." Immediately counter positions vie for attention, because even if we're being told that people don't change, we recognize that our images of them can be modified with time.

Another set of stories dealt with moments in which writers gained some insight into the dynamics of their own language behavior, either how it came to be the way it is today or the effect it has on others. One such anecdote springs from the familiar, "Oh, you teach English. I'd better watch my grammar!"

> You can take the girl out of Brooklyn but you can't take Brooklyn out of the girl.
>
> Several years ago while having a conversation with my next door neighbor, I noticed that she was eyeing me strangely.
>
> "What's wrong?" I asked.
>
> "Did you hear what you said?" was her shocked reply.
>
> "What are you talking about?" At this point I was rather annoyed.
>
> "You said 'gonna,' and you're an English teacher," she replied.
>
> I was really annoyed. I didn't think that I had to watch my words while engaging in everyday conversation. As a matter of fact that particular expression was part of my everyday speech. I suppose I grew up speaking like that throughout my childhood in New York.
>
> Yes, my neighbor made me so self-conscious that I catch myself every time I say "gonna" and I do say it more often than I should.

And immediately a larger issue is pointed to: the sudden realization that people respond to us in terms of our social role, not just for ourselves.

The next account elaborates in more detail the writer's growing sensitivity to dialect differences and their power in determining how people judge us:

> Until I became a transplanted Southerner, teaching in an eastern Montana high school, I had never been aware of my southwestern, specifically Pike County, Arkansas, dialect. It was probably because I had never been around any "foreigners," unless I could count Camille Yore, the senior from Chicago, who was my dorm counselor when I was a sophomore in Holcombe Hall at the University of Arkansas in 1960.
>
> I grew up thinking, I suppose, that everybody either talked the way kin and friend did or they talked "proper." "Proper" was the definitive word the kids in Daisy used to label the affected tone, pronunciation, and vocabulary picked up by kids whose families traveled north to Indiana for the tomato harvest every year. Those kids would return from Huntington every late fall saying things like "youse guys" instead of "y'all," causing all of the rest to us to titter uncontrollably. For a few weeks after their return, their language sounded "proper" to us (which today I interpret as meaning "affected" or high-toned. And I remember that as a kid, you just didn't want to talk "proper." Somebody might think you were stuck-up).
>
> But that's really background. The point I need to make is that no one—teacher, college prof, or friend—at home in Arkansas ever prepared me (maybe they didn't know) for the culture shock I would experience when I began teaching in Glasgow, Montana. My upbringing was strict. Daddy and Mama (all adults really) expected

kids (especially *girls*) to be extremely well-behaved. Among the requirements were the proper responses to questions requiring "yes" or "no" answers, i.e., "yes, ma'am," "no, ma'am," "yes, sir," and "no, sir."

As a student teacher and a regular, salaried teacher in Arkansas, I had never had any problem with having my students respond similarly to me. But then, I was in the first stages of my career. It never occurred to me that I would have any difficulty in requiring the same type of responses from my students in Glasgow. After all, kids were kids.

Admittedly, it *was* hard. My little eighth graders in Glasgow had heard relatively few people talk the way I did. I say *few* due to the fact that the United States Air Force had situated a military base some twenty miles north of the little town and all the military dependents (kids) attended Glasgow Public Schools. Since the school was largely populated with kids who had come to Montana from all points East, West, South, and North, I wasn't a complete oddity.

My error in insisting that my students adopt/respect/practice my peculiar language/dialect patterns came to light when one of my eighth graders shyly confided to me that after responding "yes, ma'am" and "no, ma'am" to me daily in class she had "slipped" and responded similarly to her mother who was promptly offended, suspicious that her daughter was trying to be fresh. My student was upset because she was confused as to how one way of speaking would be acceptable, in fact, required by one person while being perfectly unacceptable to another.

I was immediately empathetic with the girl and from that day became gradually more willing to blend in with the culture I lived in at the moment. Little did I know that I would encounter additional problems and humorous times in Maine and in New York State all due to my dialect differences. Montana was an initiation, but it was far from being the end of the story.

Notice how this story functions like a motif in the ongoing score of the writer's life. Montana may have set the scene, but the recurrences are anticipated as she moves around the country. Maine and New York are already variations on her theme. Repetitions in stories are powerful signs of our common humanity.

Another teacher wrote about the powerful influence adult responses can have on the young:

"Good" Is Not Always Good for a Child

To this day I can see a blurred vision of that piece of paper and can still feel some of the anger, shame, rejection and determination I felt eighteen years ago. I learned a lot of things from that experience, some of which I have realized only since becoming a teacher myself. But I learned one lesson that day which I have not forgotten. I learned that I shouldn't write poetry.

We had been studying tropical climates. Social studies was my favorite subject and also, I think, Mrs. Jaffe's. Our social studies task for this day was to write a poem about the Amazon River. It had to be at least four lines long, had to rhyme, and had to be illustrated. I don't remember anything at all about writing the poem or the actual poem itself. But I know I copied it onto the center of the white composition paper in my very best handwriting and drew jungle pictures all around it. I know it was about the Amazon and I know it rhymed.

When we got our papers back mine had "good" written on it. There were no other comments. It was the lowest grade I had gotten all year—and it was my favorite subject. I was devastated.

It never occurred to me in fourth grade that writing a poem about the Amazon had little to do with social studies or with poetry. It didn't occur to me to ask Mrs. Jaffe why my poem was "good" rather than "excellent" or, at least, "very good." It didn't (thank goodness) lessen my interest in social studies. But I have never since wanted to write poetry.

In recounting such incidents we see more clearly the kind of impact a teacher might have: how as children we invest the world of adults with a judgmental authority to which those in power are all too frequently oblivious.

"A Reading Lesson" points in at least two directions. It raises questions regarding literacy and its power, and also offers the age-old loss of innocence tale in which our idealized image of a revered adult is shattered when we see a significant flaw:

A Reading Lesson

At about the age of eleven, the importance and power of being able to decode and encode the written word was poignantly brought home to me. A favorite aunt who had spent her life as a skilled and highly paid seamstress in charge of finishing tuxedos mentioned that she had never learned to read or write. I was surprised by the revelation and couldn't believe that such a talented and entertaining person hadn't mastered these basic skills. It baffled me that such a great storyteller had never been able to read or express her marvelous wit in writing. How could this reasonably prosperous and bright person lack a skill that most ordinary fourth graders have mastered?

My consternation was imparted when an attempt to start her on the road to reading ended in frustration. I made several futile attempts to have her read a three-word sentence that appeared in a primary reader that I had at home. I can still vividly recall the way she labored to read the sentence "Here I go." I remember offering to pronounce the first word for her. After giving her the first word she proudly read the rest of the sentence as "Here e joe."

I did my best to conceal the shock and disappointment that I felt. Shaken by the events of the day, I made my mind up to never be as vulnerable as I now perceived my aunt to be.

Our response here is already influenced by the artistic or rhetorical resources of language. "*A* Reading Lesson" is really "*the* reading lesson" in terms of the impact on the author, but by keeping the indefinite article, the initial unsuspecting and unassuming innocence is maintained, and thus the later moment of revelation is made more powerful by contrast.

As they record our observations of human phenomena, stories store up the data that will later form the basis for the implicit theories we use to explain the social world. Some of these have to do with our notions about how young children develop language and ideas. Are they passive receptors of what we tell them? Or are they already actively putting together bits and pieces of experience according to their personal sense configurations before testing them publicly? One mother's brief account offers evidence on this matter:

Nathan is my two-and-a-half-year-old son whose mind and body are accumulating many memories. As we walked out the door yesterday we paused on the back porch. Looking up at us, his gaze looking alive, was a small mouse, his body dented by a steel bar across his back. He had been trapped the night before by the stove in our kitchen and had been removed to the porch by my eldest son whose desire it was to alarm all people departing by the back steps.

Nathan kneeled down to examine the mouse. "Hi, mouse! Oh . . . Oh dear. The mouse is broken. Poor mouse." Nathan sat in an Asian squat, his hands clutching each other out of a mixture of fear and respect for this frozen but friendly little animal. The mouse looked back at Nathan whose eyes grew with the examination. "Hi, mouse. You hurt? Too bad." Nathan looked up at me, his face a caricature of sympathy. "Mommy, the mouse is broken. Fix him."

Later on, Nathan asked me a question. "Who builded me?" Not sure how to respond, I answered: "God, Daddy and I did." It was not the right answer because Nathan asked again. "No, I mean when I was apart . . . who put me together?" "Who do you think put you together when you were apart?" Nathan had the answer to his own question. "I did."

Nathan is learning about the relationship between his linguistic categories and the death of the mouse. Further, we see him overgeneralizing the syntactic rules of English to form "builded." In telling this story, the mother not only further asserts her relationship with her son, she's also forming her concept of how children develop and of what characterizes their intellectual capacities even at this early age.

The world isn't always as benign and rational a place as the stories so far have pictured it. One teacher describes a jarring experience that occurred while he was driving along peacefully in his automobile:

> While driving east in the middle lane of the Long Island Expressway, I noticed, in my rear-view mirror, that a car was coming up very fast. Since I was doing 50-55 MPH I decided to get into the right lane to let this car pass, even though the traffic was extremely light and no cars were in the left lane.
>
> So I signaled and looked behind me and started over. I looked in my mirror as I did so and saw the car almost on me, but it too was going into the right lane! It was trying to pass me on the right, even though the left lane was empty, and the driver assumed I was staying in the middle. At the last second the car zoomed around me and passed me in the middle lane. As he passed me in his souped-up, raised-rear-suspension car, he slowed enough to look over and make motions at me with his hands, as if *I* were in the wrong. I could see his face, his mouth no doubt emptying obscenities at me. At that point I was so angry and rattled that I raised my left hand off the steering wheel and extended my middle finger in his direction.
>
> That drove him to a frenzy. He zoomed around and directly in front of my car and then slammed his brakes on so that I would have hit his rear if I had not slammed my brakes on as quickly. He kept this up, brakes on and off for a few seconds, while my heart pounded in my throat. At this point I was cursing at the top of my lungs at this maniac ahead of me who apparently didn't care if we had an accident, as long as he got even. He kept looking back at me as he slowed down and speeded up, while I made circular motions at my temple with my right index finger, while blasting my horn with my other hand on the steering wheel. After a few minutes of this (probably seconds, but they seemed like minutes), he roared off at what must have been 75 or 80 MPH.

How do we account for such deviant behavior? How quickly we can change from our civilized selves when the irrational descends upon us. Our patterned lives risk being shattered when persistently disrupted by unexplained "frenzy." In the stories we later tell, we seek respite by reasserting our sanity and attempting to explain our outbursts of disorder.

From Story to Poem

Our need to craft linguistically can transform unrehearsed tales into art. Our first linguistic encounter with an experience may be self-expressive, but our natural concern for form, sound and rhythm may urge us into more artistic modes. The first telling of a story already contains the germ of art which, if we choose, can be nourished further into some more deliberately crafted structure, both of language and ideas. As we revise to attain more pleasing forms, we begin to notice how the aesthetic shapes of the story reinforce the delicate balance of values we're exploring. In telling the story initially we sort out its signficiances. In retellings, our concerns become clearer and the story's artistic character begins to assume a more central focus. The immediate event begins to reverberate with universal qualities. In the story's repetitions, character is more finely delineated, themes more strikingly or subtly highlighted, and the language more carefully polished.

Our natural inclination to tell stories and then refine and modify their form can become a key to motivating writing. In young children, the narrative will be their first extended discourse in speech, and getting the words down on paper can be just a step away. Being able to capture their stories in words and pictures makes children enthusiatic about writing. Because students need legitimate reasons to write, stories provide the obvious entry into the writing cycle. Stories provide the initial sense of urgency which the writer requires; and the individual story builds momentum, a sustaining desire, which can impel the writer to further shape and revise the language of expression. Habits of mind developed in narration then can transfer to exposition.

Consider the first story about the student's crush on her English teacher now that the writer has tightened the narrative line into a crisp six stanza poem:

I wanted you
even with your
buck teeth and that
old jalopy
you called a car.

you'd drive me home
on cold days. the
heater never
worked, but i looked
at you and burned.

your eyes scolded
my flirtations:
"don't, for christ's sake;

i'm your teacher,
and you're sixteen!"

you'd stop the car
to dismiss me.
but nights i dreamed
of rumblings in
your rumble seat.

we met again
years later. you'd
married a pale,
slight nun, in white
up to her chin.

you shared eight kids,
two dogs, and a
station wagon.
and you'd never
had your teeth fixed.

Turned into art, the tale is now stripped to its essence and begins to resound powerfully with our own remembrances of adolescence.

In this movement toward the universal, not only is the reader offered an artifact of deeper emotional significance, but the writer also has had the opportunity to test her potential to push her language to its limits. In the opening and closing stanzas, "teeth" begins and ends a cycle; words begin to work at multiple levels. The concatenation of "heater" with "burned" evokes an image of adolescent passion. And how appropriate is the fire/ice contrast that sets the literal context for the scene: trying to keep warm on a cold day. Even the jalopy's heating failure parallels the teacher's, and thus our picture and comprehension of the vividness of an adolescent's emotional fantasy life are intensified.

Journals: Our Initial Story Repository

The record of observation and insight that is possible when we keep a journal serves a variety of learning purposes and may appear in multiple forms and styles. As documents of our unrehearsed language and ideas, journals exist at a stage of pre-art or pre-exposition and thus, for the most part, are for the writer's eyes only. As Thoreau once remarked, "The journal is a record of experience and growth, not a preserve of things well done or said." Our journal entries are notes or epistles to ourselves, for frequently they'll leave other readers bewildered; only the writer holds the key to the gaps and hidden references in the imperfect linguistic constructions. Still, the writer's natural language rhythms can be released in the journal's unconstrained writing environment. Journals often yield prose and poetry of surprising power. From Samuel Pepys to Anne Frank the journal has followed an honorable tradition in our culture, allowing writers to listen in on themselves, while providing readers with records of the meaning-making mind in action.

Joyce Carol Oates comments on the role of the journal in the formation and evolution of her own thought:

> "I began keeping a formal journal several years ago. It resembles a sort of ongoing letter to myself, mainly about literary matters. What interests me in the process of my own experience is the wide range of my feelings. For instance, after I finish a novel I tend to think of the experience of having written it as being largely pleasant and challenging. But in fact (for I keep careful records) the experience is various. I do suffer temporary bouts of frustration and inertia and depression . . . . Afterward, however, I simply forget. My feelings crystallize (or are mythologized) into something much less complex. All of us who keep journals do so for different reasons, I suppose, but we must have in common a fascination with the surprising patterns that emerge over the years—a sort of arabesque in which certain elements appear and reappear, like the designs in a well-wrought novel. The voice of my journal is very much like the one . . . in which I think or meditate when I'm not writing fiction.
>
> (Joyce Carol Oates, *Writers at Work* 5th Series)

Without such written records the range of pattern recognition pointed to by Oates would be greatly diminished owing to the tendency of our memories to keep dissolving as we move to the next pressing moment in our lives. Until we're forced or force ourselves to set down our present response to the phenomena we're currently experiencing, we don't really know the direction or purposes toward which our thoughts are working. The same holds true for both our emotional and intellectual capacities. A series of journal entries about a growing relationship, for instance, will begin to reveal the subtle contours of our sympathies. We gain perspective by recognizing, through their recurrence, how our characteristic responses take shape in the midst of similar situations.

So, too, a journal entry in which we reflect on our first encounter with the concept of subatomic particles creates both a benchmark for us to judge future learning in physics and an opportunity to begin connecting the discipline's specialized vocabulary to our own. We never receive knowledge passively; rather, we must work at mastering and reconstruing facts and theories about the world. The journal frees us from the limitations of memory and fosters our ability to "shape at the point of utterance." It is increasingly being recognized by teachers as a central tool for learning and for stimulating the imagination.

Summary of Journal Functions

1. *Recording* Learner sets down perceived information or events.
2. *Responding* Learner gives immediate reactions to subject content or events.
3. *Questioning* Learner questions the structures, meanings, and implications of the subject's content or the lived-through or observed events.
4. *Rehearsing* Learner practices a role or "tries on" a new language by using the jargon, syntax, and persona which characterize the subject.
5. *Connecting* Learner links event or the content of the subject area with other phenomena being experienced.
6. *Consolidating* Learner summarizes and interrelates the abstract concepts and systems that make up the discipline or are embedded in the experienced story.
7. *Anticipating* Learner speculates on what events may come next or where the learning in the discipline is heading.
8. *Inventing* Learner creates stories, concepts, relationships, or insights not previously in his repertoire.
9. *Analyzing and Synthesizing the Teaching/Learning Process* Learner comments on the strategies and forms of the teaching and learning that relate to the subject being studied.
10. *Analyzing and Synthesizing the Composing Process* Learner details and reflects on his own process of writing or on how he thinks or acts in terms of the creative aspects of any other discipline or art form.

Note: In any given entry more than one function may be occurring.

Journals: The Teacher's Response and Responsibility

The journal contains that writing which is closest to the self. It offers a valuable opportunity to experiment and thus make mistakes, free of the judgmental eye of the teacher. Because public evaluation has nothing to do with journal writing, the writer need pay only subsidiary attention to the conventions of writing. Also, the contexts for establishing or recovering the referents to people, objects or places mentioned in an entry need not be carefully attended to. This doesn't mean that removing the pressure of formal conventions will lead to muddle and chaos, for finally the writer will have some stake in being able to comprehend his own entries. It simply means that such a relaxed setting frequently encourages invention. What we then set down in a journal may range from mere notes of our ideas and observations to preliminary drafts of what may later be revised for a specific audience beyond ourselves.

In this respect, teachers can play a crucial, if gentle, role as encouraging reader. It's necessary to establish that although you have asked students to keep journals, you're not required to read and comment on every entry, nor must they fill up the pages of their journals on any lockstep routine basis. Once the environment for sharing give-and-take exists, students will solicit your response to certain entries that are of particular importance to them while requesting that others not be read. This depends upon trust, but you can begin establishing your own credibility by sharing your journal habits with your students. This could include letting them see you write in your journal during a time set aside for them to write in theirs. You can also read them selections from your journal, welcoming their responses, both oral and written. Such modeling, though it may feel somewhat risky or uncomfortable at first, demonstrates conclusively that you believe in the merits of keeping a journal and aren't simply pawning off another busywork assignment on them.

When you respond in writing to your students' journals, do so personally, not with rubber stamp phrases. Say, "This makes me think of . . . ," or "I liked how you connected this with . . . ," or "Had you thought of . . . ," rather than "Good idea," or "Keep up the good work," or "Try harder next time." Your comments are meant to be a dialogue, not an evaluative monologue, so what you write is what you'd say if you were chatting with the student. This back-and-forth approach makes it natural for a student to write future journal entries which have been stimulated by your questions and comments.

One key to guaranteeing the success of journals in your classroom is to be relaxed. Don't overwhelm students with the task, but allow it to develop organically, letting it work for them in ways they discover. By encouraging and gently prodding, and by putting your own writing up front, journal writing can open up new learning channels in your curriculum.

Journals in Action

When students, even young ones, have the opportunity to jot down their understandings of course content, teachers have an effective means of gauging what learning is taking place. The journal catches more than just right answers; it also provides room for the underlying processes. With such knowledge of how the students' learning is progressing, the teacher can adjust and react accordingly. Consider the following journal entries written by sixth graders who were pursuing a social studies unit on the Renaissance:

> I think it is kind of good that people stuck with what they believed in. If there was no Renaissance period we just might still be like people in

the Middle Ages. Maybe, maybe not. I think that the church was too powerful, even in the Renaissance. How the Middle Ages lasted so long before the Renaissance is *beyond* me. I think Popes used their power very unwisely. (—12-year-old girl)

* * *

It was a time that I think everyone was happy. Wouldn't you be happy getting off the dumb manor system? I was wondering where the people lived. I wanted to know if their homes were above or in back of their shops. It must have been a fun time. When I see commercials for the Ren. faire everyone looks happy. I think I know mainly what the Ren. was like. (—12-year-old girl)

* * *

I think the Renaissance was a much different kind of time from any other time. I learned that the Middle Ages was a much crumier time to live in then the Renaissance time. People had much more freedom during the Renaissance and they didn't have to work like the serfs.
I also learned that religion wasn't as important as man was, during the Ren. time (—11-year-old girl)

* * *

The Renaissance began when man began to question things he didn't understand and think of life on earth more than after death. Other men started to explore unknown lands, conquer it, set up colonies there, and to trade with the east. Feudal estates died, towns grew up, and a whole new type of life began in Europe. (—12-year-old girl)

The generalizations contained in these entries indicate that these students are accurately interacting with ideas the teacher has presented. Furthermore, their own personal responses, questions, and connections enrich the learning process. One girl makes a connection with commercials for a local Renaissance Fair, another contrasts the "crumier" Middle Ages, a third wonders why the Renaissance didn't come sooner. In each case, the teacher can expand her students' inquiry with her own responses to the journals. And certainly the teacher reading and responding to these entries, especially *during* a unit, has a much better idea of how effective her teaching is than if she simply waited for the results of a final examination.

In another sixth grade social studies unit covering some concepts in economics, one journal entry shows how a student actively practices relating terminology to concepts:

> I understand that Life Expectancy means how long you are going to live. That's all I understand about that. Infant Mortality, what a funny word. Infant means baby or small child, but mortality means how long a baby is going to live. Why don't they just say Child or Baby Expectancy it'd be a lot easier. Japan has the lowest Infant Mortality because it has a large G. N. P.? Literacy means can you read and write. Your not supposed to confuse literacy with being smart or dumb. Russia has a lot of literacy? Population means how many people in an area. They have 9,000,000 on the island they call Japan. No wonder the people are so little.

Here the student exhibits his reasoning ability by critiquing "infant mortality" and remarking on the relationship between population density and a people's physical size. This connection, however spurious, could be the basis of much investigation, testing, and subsequent writing were the teacher to ask something like: "Does this mean people in a crowded city are smaller than people living on a farm?" or "Do children grow up smaller if they live in an apartment building than if they live in a big suburban house?" The student would then need to delve into demographics, physiology, and possibly other appropriate disciplines. The density/size connection might also be used to persuade the student to develop a short story in which characters change according to the environments they find themselves in.

Journal entries can show the teacher where she still has to go with her teaching:

> I didn't learn much but I did learn something thow it is one big blerr. If you have a bad GNP there would be Infant Mortality which would cut down population I can't get the rest. What I don't get is how it all ties in and how life expectancy and infant morality have to do with globel problems.

* * *

> I learned that countries with a high G.N.P. are countries with lower infant mortality, longer life expectancy, higher literacy, and pretty well controlled population. These countries, since they have a high G.N.P. they can afford good medical care, good education and good scientific knowledge and investigations. (I don't understand Peter R.) The unit is easy and educational, but boring. I hope that later in the unit we start some projects to do in *class.*

The first student suggests that she's overwhelmed by the ideas and can't connect them with "globel problems." The second student feels free to comment on the overall teaching/learning strategies used in the unit. Quite simply she was bored. Whether or not the teacher covers all the information she wants through some in-class project format, the journals at least keep her informed of the achievements and attitudes of her students, which traditional procedures fail to take into account.

These learning logs and the direct assessments they provide aren't limited to English or social studies. Math and science afford equal opportunities for rehearsal and idea exploration. In their math journals, these same sixth graders demonstrate that much more is going on in their heads than just adding sums:

> I think 77-78 is the best math year I've had, sure. I sit next to real goof-offs but I still get my work done. Math is may favorite academic course so far this year.
>
> Although I like what we've been doing, I think we, as a class, should spend more time on real life situations. This checking unit is the idea I'm referring to, but we should also do income taxes forms and other such materials.
>
> We should try to put math to a pratical use, (no offense intended) I would guess 80% of the class does not know how to apply math to real-life problems. Instead we know 9x9=81. when what we ought to know is how to apply math concepts to real life situations.—(12-year-old boy)

* * *

> The one thing I have been doing in math for the last 7 years is making careless mistakes. Thats why I might get a bad grade on an easy test. I have been trying to work slower, hopeing that would help stop my carelessness. Do you have any other suggestions?
>
> Math is usually one of my better subjects. I really like the unit we are doing now. It is lots of fun. I am really getting tired of multiplication.
>
> —(11-year-old girl)

* * *

> So, you want to know about primes, do you? Well, lets just only work on the primes between 1-12. A prime is a number in which no other numbers can be multiplied to make that number besides 1 and itself.
>
> Here is the number 8. 8 is *not* prime.
>
> You know the factors of 8.
>
> 1, 2, 4, 8 2 x 4 and 4 x 2
> 1 x 8 and 8 x 1

You see that 2 x 4 and 4 x 2 goes into eight.

But 11 is a prime number. No other factors besides 1 and 11 can make 11.

$$1 \times 11 = 11 \qquad 11 \times 1 = 11$$

So, you see that eleven is prime because only itself times 1 equals it.

—(11-year-old boy)

These insights into learning styles and needs yield valuable information. By putting it in his own words the 11-year-old proves that he knows the concept of prime number. The girl making "careless mistakes" can be helped because she's initiating the call for help. And perhaps this teacher will go on to offer more "real life" connections in mathematics.

Process Journals

There are no formulas for journal writing; indeed, new forms and purposes keep emerging. Besides providing insight into what students are learning and their reactions to the teaching/learning climate established in the classroom, journals can be used to study the very process of writing itself. Diane Burkhardt, an innovative eighth grade teacher on Long Island who has made writing an integral part of her curriculum, recently instituted writing process journals in her class. The results were startling, demonstrating the depth of self-awareness and honesty young people possess. Here's a page from her own journal describing some of her apprehensions about the project:

> I have been obsessed with process journals throughout the weekend. I watched very little of the Super Bowl!!!
>
> The feeling I've had is a very good one. I have worked with a passion for the task. I was pleasantly surprised by what several kids had written . . . very touched at some of what was shared.
>
> I've had little sleep but feel tremendous energy. I've been driven to read and respond quite carefully/thoroughly to all the what-I-know-about-myself-as-a-writer pieces and then to look for a variety of entries to publish? I guess I'm waging war or something, but with guerrilla tactics rather than heavy artillery.
>
> One of the forces driving me has been my desire to be ready first thing tomorrow with some examples of entries and p.j.'s to return. I'm ready and that feels good.
>
> Must not get hopes too high for "results." It's a personal and individual thing for each kid.

Here she considers how to share with her entire class representative excerpts from student journals. Her class had already been divided into peer writing groups, and she wanted to show them how important a collaborative community is in fostering the whole writing enterprise. Her decision to "publish" selections from their journals wasn't made without risk. Diane was wary of violating the sense of trust she'd built. Though she was gratified with what the students had written, she didn't want to foster any false comparisons among student entries.

The relaxed and reassuring tone Diane uses to introduce "Excerpts from Process Journals" emphasizes her concern with creating an atmosphere of openness in her classroom, where individual achievement is valued and respected but not allowed to overwhelm those who may not succeed as well on a particular writing task:

Cover Sheet for Excerpts from Process Journals

Remember when you read this that they are from a lot of different people's process journals—*all* of them are your classmates.

The purpose is only to share a variety of entries. These are *not* meant to show "the right way" of writing process entries. The only "right way" is the way that works for you and is truly helpful to you.

You have a choice between making it work for you or doing it just as an assignment—more homework . . . a drag . . . a chore.

One of the problems with presenting typed examples is that they may appear too neat. Process journals are *not* final drafts!! Concern with neatness and correctness of your process journal entries draws your energy away from ideas and feelings.

ENJOY READING. I ENJOYED PUTTING THIS TOGETHER.

Diane Burkhardt

The issue of trust was paramount among Diane's students and is reflected in their entries. This trust can never be overemphasized, and she models it frequently by showing her class that she trusts them enough to solicit their responses to her own work. When the right accepting climate doesn't exist, students either clam up or write self-protectively. The reciprocity of trust is the key, as the final entry reveals; but it required Diane's continual urging and encouragement in the face of initial student skepticism:

Student Journal Entries

1. I would never tell anybody somebody else's feelings because I know how it feels when you think that you can trust someone and then they turn around and tell everyone what you told them.

2. I would feel good if someone respected me and trusted me enough to share . . . I will definitely respect other people's writing . . . If someone tells me something very private, I can't tell anybody else about it because it makes me feel guilty . . . . I can trust my group if I share it . . . . I would not laugh unless I'm supposed to laugh . . . . I need honesty, trust, and someone that will listen and not laugh . . . . I think I am honest and I know I can respect other people's writing no matter what it is . . . . I don't think anyone should be laughed at when they read their piece because I know how much it hurts when my piece is rejected.
3. I'm definitely sure I can treat the other people in my group the same way I would like them to treat me. If I couldn't, then why should they have to treat me good? I think everyone wants this trust.
4. I need to know that the piece will stay within the group and I feel that if I want it that way others would want it that way and I would respect that and keep it within the group.
5. When I wrote about trust last night, I thought I could only trust ____. *Now* I think I could trust my writing group. We just have to be willing to risk.
6. I was so involved in listening to people in class that I forgot I was there. Everyone seemed so serious and mature. I changed my opinions of some classmates for the better.
7. All of a sudden the thought came to my head that all it takes for me to be trusted is to trust others. Is it really that simple? Is that all you are saying? All I have to do is risk. Yes, I can do that.

Once over the trust barrier, students showed a remarkable willingness to write and great sensitivity in being able to express how they went about it:

> I tried to write an ending. I can't get one. I've started 4 different times each time it starts out a different way. All end no where. It's really pissing me off. I want it to end with Brian talking Tony out of it. But out of what? I can't think of what I want Brian and Jennie to say. Maybe I'll just change the whole thing. Not even have Jeannie and Brian come at all. But then how will Jo get out of it. I don't want her dead and I don't want him killing himself. I'm stuck.

* * *

> I decided to write a sports story. I decided to because it would be easier to write a sports story. I was right all along. The story never stopped rolling. From the beginning I had ideas popping out of my head. Once

the idea was all down on paper a new idea came. I discovered that what you said was true. Stick to what you know about and writing won't be so difficult and that your stories will be better.

* * *

I was sitting by a window in my bedroom and was watching the leaves fall off of the trees. I thought about how it seems like only yesterday I was watching the trees get their leaves. I then started to think about the time I was in first grade. I have no idea how I thought of this, I just did. I had a perfect picture in my head of my teacher Miss Tuthill working at the chalkboard and me at my desk. Then I began to think that I should write a story about when I was in first grade. One thing we did every morning was copy sentences. We did this *every* morning. Miss Tuthill never even let us skip a day of writing sentences. That is what I decided to write about. I had no trouble at all because I saw a picture of the scene I was writing in my head and I just wrote what I saw. With the picture I also remembered how I felt in first grade in different situations. I remembered that one day I was crying in school and I could remember what I was saying to myself at that time. (I didn't write about this though.) Even as I write this process now, details about school when I was in first grade are coming into my head. It is kind of sad to think of things and know that I will never be in first grade again.

* * *

I was starting on the other draft of the beginning of my piece last night and the ideas kept going so I kept writing. I got a beginning a middle and an end in 50 minutes. So I guess writing it in sections isn't that much of a good idea. I've got to do maybe 2 or 3 more drafts of this story.

I just read this process over and I think that I put too many extra words in a sentence if I don't think it out before I write it down.

I was pretty comfortable writing last night. I like writing big and skipping lines. I wrote neat for about the 1st two lines and then switched to sloppy print and skipping lines. It's easier for me to write this way.

* * *

It took me a long time to finish this piece 2 hours on Sun and 3 hours tonight. These hours are straight. I don't do anything but write no other homework or anything but I get up and brush my hair, write down names and words to songs talk to ___ answer the phone and talk for a little while with whoever it was. If I tell them I've got a lot of HW and they say what do you have to do and I say I've got to revise an English piece they say that's nothing but they don't know about my stories or how I like to take my time writing the piece and finally getting it completed. I left off ending on this draft I'll ask my w.g. about what I've got so far.

* * *

Argghh

too long? time wise
too much description
in some parts
too little in
others.
Too much cross
out
too sloppy
too much concern
about what other
people will think
too little concentration
too much thinking
about time
too much thinking
about game tomorrow
too much stop then
start—even while I write this
about a certain
person
Argghhh

Remember that these entries were composed by enthusiastic but otherwise average eighth graders. Yet their reflections on the joys and agonies of writing parallel those of any writer. No lock step formula will lead to this kind of writing; each student must find his own way. When let loose, these average writers exhibit great fluency. They're not bogged down by the odd mechanical error; instead, an animated rhythm informs their prose as they speak of a matter close to the self: how they create and use written language. Confident that they're protected by a blanket of trust, they are free to reveal unself-consciously their minds at work. Through process journals, Diane has unloosed boundless energy and awareness among her students that shows in the range of written work they've completed throughout the year.

Journals: A Final Note of Caution

Inevitably, journals will on occasion contain material of an extremely personal nature. Such material may pose a threat to the writer by revealing what lies beneath carefully constructed defenses. Similarly, this material may threaten us as teachers, who aren't equipped to handle every sort of personal revelation. We're not in the therapy business, so we're obliged to steer clear of therapeutic discourse.

But knowing that journals or any sort of authentic writing close to the self will be revelatory in crucial ways need not intimidate us, for to shut off genuine writing is to stifle the entire writing enterprise in advance. Rather, we must prepare a system of response and openness which encourages the writer to recognize that he's writing for a caring public, not simply burdening his readers with his personal problems. To begin with, you need to share your own journal entries, making clear that you're not revealing everything—that some of your writing addresses matters inappropriate for a larger audience. Such modeling reinforces your instruction that students identify passages not intended for your eyes. Next, the responses you write to student journals will go a long way in establishing the necessary dialogue tone that's needed if journals aren't to turn into true confession diaries. This involves responding on the basis of natural human dialogue, not setting yourself up as an all-knowing commentator seeking to analyze the psychological secrets of his students.

These cautions amount to common sense, but the issue of avoidance must always be faced squarely. It's easier never to assign journals, and thus never to risk getting material that threatens to compromise your position as the teacher. The system is filled with these kinds of safeguards-in-advance approaches and the writing that results is, not surprisingly, pretty deadly stuff. Yet, just because journal writing may produce occasionally unsettling material, fear shouldn't prevent us from using this means of enhancing the students' future writing powers. If we're to grant students the necessary control over themselves as writers, we must learn to relinquish some of our control.

By beginning with stories and journals, the teacher establishes himself as a friend of the writer, not as a transmitter of predetermined writing skills. By helping make sense of experience, stories form a bond between student and teacher, and this can extend to the journal as well. In capturing fleeting moments the journal frees the writer from time's tyranny, but in doing so it also grants dominion over content to the writer himself. The teacher must not view this transfer of authority as undermining his role in the classroom. Instead, the journal and other opportunities for narrative writing allow students to explore feelings and ideas crucial to them in a non-threatening environment. The confidence that's nurtured by a teacher's acceptance of and response to stories and journal entries helps establish that writing is a rewarding and necessary activity for subsequent academic and personal life.

WRITING TO LEARN

1. Write up a brief account of an incident which you find yourself telling others frequently. This incident may or may not have happened to you. What is the point of your story? Does it reveal any issues or themes that are important to you?
2. Write up a brief story of some incident that you remember as having influenced your language. What roles did the participants play in this incident? What specifically about your language behavior was influenced by this incident?
3. Choose some event that is looming in your future. What role will you be playing in it? What are your expectations and anxieties about it? Write a brief story imagining what this event will be like or how it will turn out. Try alternative approaches and endings if you like.
4. Now reflect on who you are and the kinds of stories you tell. How do you present yourself through stories? Does this change for different audiences? Do you seek confirmation for your stories? What happens when there is disagreement over one of your accounts? Who modifies what and why? What do your stories tell you about what is most central to you at particular phases of your life?
5. Begin keeping a journal/log if you haven't already done so. You might record events, observations, responses, and ideas. These entries may vary in form and purpose and need not be connected one to the other. Try a range of styles and see if you can discover new potential within yourself.
6. For a while at least try keeping a journal/log related to a particular learning activity you are engaged in. For instance, you might want to keep a response journal for your reading of this book and how you agree or disagree with what is said. Further, you might suggest connections with your own teaching/learning experience.
7. After keeping your journal(s) for several weeks, read back over your entries. What connections, patterns, and idiosyncracies do you discover? Had you forgotten what you said in a particular entry? What does being able to recover what was lost to immediate memory mean for you? Wherein lies the powers of keeping a journal? Who finally is its audience?

3

From the Inside Out: The Composing Process

One of the most significant developments in understanding writing and how to teach it has been research on what people do when they write. Beginning with the pioneering efforts of Janet Emig (1969), researchers have tried through various techniques to uncover the process behind the written product. While none of the research techniques have been perfect, we now know more than ever about what writers are thinking as they are writing. In this chapter we'll explain what we've learned so far about the composing process and, particularly, we'll explore its implications for teaching.

The composing process is exploratory. This is easier to see in the beginning when a writer is taken with the urge to write, but even a piece of "finished" writing may not be the end of the writer's thought on the subject. The composing process is essentially a meaning-making process. As the writer begins percolating and drafting, there's often only a vague sense of intention or purpose. The full thrust of ideas has not yet emerged and part of the cycling back and forth among percolating, drafting, and revising involves the writer in shaping purposes and refining intentions. Donald Murray (1978), one of the foremost students of this process, which he calls internal revision, has collected over 2000 statements from professional writers, all of whom essentially repeat E. M. Forster's remark: "How do I know what I think until I see what I say?"

The meaning that thus emerges from one's text, and has been the focus of rereading it, is a result of this forward-backwards motion of the composing process. This interaction—returning to reread the text from a different angle of vision—plays a key role in helping the writer push forward to create meaning.

First, the writer proceeds forward, exploring through the writing some meaning, or maybe more than one. But to ensure that meaning is being communicated, it's essential for writers to go back and read what they've written, this time to clarify their intended meaning(s). At this point, usually near the end of what we've been calling *drafting*, some reader feedback is often required. The process of communicating clearly demands that the writer know how her intended meanings are being interpreted by a reader, and even for the most experienced writer this usually requires some actual response. In many cases, the *revising* component of the process won't happen without some feedback. It's frequently reader response which provides the necessary perspective shift for the *re*-vision aspect of revising to occur.

SONDRA PERL There are two terms that I think are helpful for teachers to think about for distinguishing the two parts of the composing process. One term is "retrospective structuring." That, for me, refers to all of the backward movements in the process. They're things that do not follow any linear logic. People go back to the words on the page in order to go forward. They go back to the topic they've been given to develop it more. And they also go back to a "felt sense," a feeling they have about the topic that's not yet in words. It's a kind of vague, fuzzy intention they have. It's an intention they had at the beginning which they go back to and try to match their text to.

We can help students recognize this intention search by getting them to ask themselves: "Is this the word I want?" "Is this the phrase I want?" "Does this capture what I intend to say?" These are internal criteria. They're not related to what the teacher says is the right word. It's related to what the student feels is his word. That's the word that carries the meaning for him.

The other term, the other direction, is what I call "projective structuring." This is also a mental posture, a way writers need to take their audience into account. I see this as an outward looking, forward looking, projecting out to call up a sense of one's audience: "Who am I writing for?" "How will this person understand this?" "Can I get a sense of my reader that will help me know how to shape my text to meet that reader's demands?"

Similarly, the process of editing, which focuses attention on the surface features or conventions of standard written English, shouldn't happen alone. Every writer needs and deserves help in modifying and polishing her penultimate draft. Left on their own, even the most skilled writers will miss a comma or overlook a spelling error, and so here, too, reader feedback is crucial to success. Because a number of sub-routines make up the process of writing, a final draft takes far longer to evolve than we usually allow for in school. Teachers must therefore help students learn to expand their conception of how a text gets created.

Percolating

Percolating takes into account a writer's accumulated experiences and all of her memories of them as well as of feelings and ideas. When viewed as part of the composing process, this way of thinking about and defining percolation has important consequences. The student writer can no longer be viewed as an empty vessel whose mind must be filled with knowledge and information supplied by an outside expert before she can start to write. Instead, the writer is the expert on the subject of her own experiences and memories. The implications are far-reaching, both to the writer and the teacher. Teachers too rarely tap the enormous resources of students' experiences implied in this view of percolating. Our students must become aware that this resource is available to them. If we're committed to improving writing abilities, we must be willing to abandon the idea that our students don't know anything until we teach them something.

Practically speaking, this means we must anticipate that the initial writing will be very personal. We're asking students to call upon their own expertise about themselves to formulate a piece of writing. The assignment may be something like: "Recall an experience in your early childhood you remember vividly that might have influenced some of your behaviors to this day"; or, "Remember someone in your past who made a strong impression on you"; or, "Try to express in writing the emotions you were feeling at some significant moment in your life." It will take some time for many of them to learn to value the stuff of their own lives as something to write about, but once they do, the power and fluency of their writing will improve dramatically.

New information can be learned, in part, through writing about it, but only when a student connects the knowledge she already possesses with the new information she's attempting to learn. If we don't ask students to make connections between what's new and what's been stockpiled through experience, we're back to the empty vessel analogy, disqualifying everything they've learned before. So if we're teaching photosynthesis in science, we can ask our students to speculate in writing on their own observations about how they think plants get food. If we're teaching literature, we might get students to write about some character in a novel they have already read whose qualities are similar to those of a character in a novel we're currently studying. Or if we're teaching early 20th century history, we could ask students to interview someone they know who grew up during that time.

The point is that students must be at the center of their own learning. Whether we're asking them to write about a personal experience, or about new information, or about something they're unsure of, we need to allow them to start from where *they* are, not from where *we* are. If we don't allow them to speak with their own voices, there's little chance that we'll know whether our teaching has been successful.

JOHN MAYHER What's your feeling about personal or expressive writing as a way of increasing fluency and comfort in student writers?

JANET EMIG We're comfortable with personal writing in the elementary schools, but I think we move away from it as we get on to high school and college.

JOHN MAYHER And that's hardly a good thing, as clearly adults also spend much of their time making connections on the basis of personal language.

JANET EMIG At all ages the opportunity to write personally infuses our essays, so there's a lovely interplay. Strengths in both are enhanced by this opportunity. I know that some teachers feel uncomfortable starting with personal writing for fear that something else will develop. We're not engaged in therapy, we're engaged in the learning and teaching of writing. But as teachers we're always focusing on the emerging text, or at least we should be, not on the person. It's the expression of a person that finds its way into a text. And that makes it a different kind of endeavor.

What better way then to begin writing than by talking about the possibilities beforehand? There are no conscious grammatical restrictions or special conventions. We don't have to worry about paragraphs, where to punctuate, or what words to capitalize. It's not permanent, so most of us don't get hung up on evaluation. Thinking through talking is a much more natural process than thinking through writing. Talk stimulates more talk: when we hear other people responding to what we say—immediate feedback—we formulate answers and respond. Ideas, feelings, thoughts that might never have occurred to us pop into mind during conversation, because someone provokes us to talk further. Talk can be the best initiator for writing if we understand it as part of percolating. (It must, of course, be purposeful, not just random chatter.)

It's essential that students feel free to write down their own interpretations of a literary selection. Sharing ideas first by talking about them gives students a better idea about what their fellow students/readers thought about the selection. By discussing their ideas, they learn how to put and defend their points of view. They can begin to spell out the reasons for their beliefs and test them against the group response before committing them to paper. And what they say can be translated into writing. "Writing" it first in talk makes it less threatening to put it in writing.

Two other percolating activites should be mentioned: note-taking (list-making) and brainstorming. If personal experiences and talk don't seem to stimulate some students into writing, brainstorming might. Talk and personal experiences make the writer the focus of attention, but brainstorming seems to change that, especially if done in pairs or groups. Everyone is contributing ideas, no one need take total responsiblity. Once ideas are written down in a brainstorming session, it's easier for some students to come up with their own later, or to find one or two to use in their writing.

Note-taking works better in situations which involve a less personal voice: in an essay, where writers need to support their ideas with outside sources. Here it's a way of keeping track of information. Note-taking can also be a valuable tool for organizing ideas at the beginning of the composing process. Writing thoughts down randomly can help later on to guide the writer in choosing where to place ideas, omit material, or add information.

Some writers use brainstorming and/or note-taking all the time; others never see the need. Because the composing process is so idiosyncratic, it makes no sense to force a writer to use either strategy. Best to let the writer do what's most comfortable. If something in the composing process isn't working right, suggest the use or elimination of one or more of these techniques.

Finally, we must acknowledge that not every writing assignment requires an elaborate formal starter activity or gimmick. Every writer brings to the act of writing her whole life, and the problem is more often one of selecting which idea best fits than of generating wholly new ideas. This, in part, is what Britton means by shaping at the point of utterance, which provides a natural transition to drafting. Writing, like talking, actually happens at that crucial moment when the words are being formed (or said) in a linear sequence. This moment calls upon all of our linguistic, cognitive, experiential, affective, and even motor skills. Everything is working together, but it's important to remember that the mechanisms themselves are functioning completely out of awareness. What we're focusing on is the meaning we're trying to make. How we start to do that is where we must now turn.

JOHN MAYHER You've suggested that shaping at the point of utterance is meant to indicate that the process of writing is a spontaneous one. It doesn't have to be over-prepared; in fact, it might be useful if we could make writing more like speech.

JAMES BRITTON We all shape at the point of utterance. Just as we're doing now. In ordinary speech we push the boat out and hope it will land somewhere, not just anywhere, but somewhere on a journey—arriving at a destination. And I think there's a kind of social pressure when you undertake to contribute to a conversation; you're claiming to have something to say and, therefore, there's social pressure on you to say it and to make sense. And I think it means that we often arrive in speech at solutions to problems that maybe we've brooded about without any success before trying to express them. And that is what I also want to encourage in writing

JOHN MAYHER In other words, if writing is made too deliberate a process, you don't think it works?

JAMES BRITTON Right. I think that spontaneity is an important part of invention and invention is what makes writing a means of learning.

Drafting

A draft, as defined by the *Oxford American Dictionary,* is "a rough preliminary written version." The key words in this definition are "rough" and "preliminary." Both imply a state of writing not yet complete, polished. If there's only one thing we can help students do to improve their writing, it should be to accustom them to producing draft versions.

Not every piece of writing requires more than one version; most journal entries and free-writing exercises are never read by anyone other than the writer. Such writings are drafts. There's no external demand for correct surface form, and they reflect the preliminary thoughts of writers on their subject. There are times when a writer will choose to expand a piece of free-writing or a journal entry into a longer, more thought-out piece. But generally, these types of writing are not developed further and we should not force our students to polish them.

The teacher's role in drafting should never be evaluative. In order to get students to see the value of drafting, they must first perceive that a draft isn't a final version. Students associate the final version with red pen corrections and a grade, so they try to be neat when they anticipate such a response. The only way that students will produce work that is "rough" and "preliminary" is if the teacher both models and encourages this process. Drafts, however, must be clearly linked with "improved" final pieces to validate the process. The sub-routines involved should be pointed out if the stusent is to realize the value of the original "mess."

If we're not to grade or correct punctuation, what is our role at the drafting stage? Quite simply, we must be supportive, ask questions and suggest possible alternatives, anything from "That sounds good, I know just what you mean" to "I don't understand this line, could you run it by me again?" or, "Maybe it would sound better if you scratched these two paragraphs." Responses of this kind are totally non-evaluative. Their purpose is to get the student to think about ways of improving the draft in a revised version. It's extremely important to be positive—to communicate to the writer that something in her draft is worth saving, may even be very good. The more strengths we can find, especially at the beginning, the more we encourage the drafting process and make clear that revision doesn't amount to starting all over again. There will be words, sentences, and paragraphs that can be left virtually unchanged from draft to final writing. Learning this will give students the positive reinforcement essential to convincing them of the importance of draft writing.

A problem that can arise with even the most constructive response from a teacher is that the student will give it undue weight, producing a paper the teacher seems to want rather than voicing her original intentions. This "psyching out" of teachers is common enough, but teacher responses on drafts can make it more likely. Ironically, the student who tries most conscientiously to follow a teacher's advice may end up damaging the paper, since the teacher may be wrong about what it needs. Students should be encouraged to seek and use reader feedback, but we can't forget that the paper is theirs. They own it. Their ideas are being expressed. They have to be the final judge of how it's supposed to sound.

SONDRA PERL Teachers have often taught writing by getting students to write; then having them hand in the paper; and finally responding to what is considered a finished draft. But all the jumble is still there. What I'm talking about is responding all along the line. We don't wait until the paper gets handed in. We get students to talk first about their ideas and talk about them in a group. We get them to free write, we get them to do a draft, or a paragraph, and bring that to the group. And we get the group to respond to the paper while it's not yet fully developed. I think that once a paper is fully written, there's some degree of commitment to it, some degree of, "This is what I've written and I don't want to change it." What I'm talking about is reversing the process: having students use each other as collaborators to think through, to help in the formulation process. If they can say to each other, "I don't understand what you're saying," then maybe they can untangle it long before it's all on the page, "engraved," set in stone.

Revising

Unless student writers have produced draft versions of their writing, they will not be successful at revising. Without appropriate response to a draft, students will take revision to mean proofreading or, worse, copying over (often reproducing the same spelling errors contained in the original draft.) Revising or *re*-vision means taking another look, to see again what has already been seen, but this time from a different perspective. That perspective shift could result from reader responses to the original draft, or it could grow out of the different appearance a draft takes after it's been set away for a day or longer. After reading the draft, the writer may decide to remove whole chunks and substitute new writing. She may discover that apart from reader responses, there were things she had written down or talked about during the percolating that she had forgotten to include in the draft, but now finds will strengthen the writing. Or she might discover that she needs more information.

As Linda Flower points out in her distinction between writer- and reader-based prose, in drafting, writers often tell the story or make their points from their own perspective ("I found this . . . ," or "I replied . . ."), while in the finished piece the reader may need other points of emphasis or organizing strategies. The writer's initial absorption then with getting her ideas down on paper—the essence of drafting—must now shift somewhat to making them clear to a reader.

JOHN MAYHER Writers have to realize that the first thing they write down isn't the only thing they're ever going to write, which means the key issue here is revision.

LINDA FLOWER Yes. I see writer-based prose as a necessary fact of life. The next step is really transforming your writing for a reader. Unfortunately, many students don't realize that they should be taking that step. And I think that's really the issue: that they don't see revision as a normal part of the composing process that anybody goes through when they have something complicated to say to someone else.

JOHN MAYHER What can writing teachers get out of this when they're trying to improve the writing strategies of their students? How can one move toward eventually producing reader-based prose?

LINDA FLOWER Two things stand out for me: one is simply helping students have a greater awareness that they have processes they have some conscious control over. That they, in fact, make choices.

> And two involves actively teaching better strategies: we can teach students planning, techniques for organizing beyond outlining, and strategies for editing. In other words, turn our knowledge about what expert writers do into teachable strategies that the rest of us can really use.

In order to do this and produce a substantial revision, the writer must be able to re-see the whole picture as well as the indiviudal parts. That is, revision is not mere editing or proofreading. We're not yet asking students to check their punctuation, look for subject-verb agreement, or watch for capitalization. We're asking that while they revise, they work on organization and clarity, that it's now time for the writing to be shaped into a cohesive structure. That's why we ask questions about paragraphs when reading a student's draft, and why in revising the student might rearrange, omit, or add paragraphs. The student has now reached the point where the writing should clearly reflect its purpose and audience. That's why we ask for more information in drafting, and why in revising the writer might add dialogue, flesh out a character, provide specific detail.

If through drafting we're exploring, discovering, and creating meaning, then in revising we're ensuring that the intended meaning is the one we're communicating. This doesn't mean that meaning can't change from draft to final writing. One consequence of revising is that writers may decide to alter meaning. In answering questions posed in drafting, or in her own rereading, the writer might decide, for example, that she doesn't have enough information to support an argument, or that she really believes in the opposing view and has many more convincing statements to make for it. When a writer discovers that the responses to her writing have generally begun, "What do you mean by . . . ?" she should understand that her meaning has not been clear. In revising, the writer can make her meaning clearer by responding to such questions, or she can return at this point to more percolating before tackling the process again.

When writing is viewed as a construction (of meaning) process, all of composing must be seen as contributing to that construction. Consequently, one revision may not be enough. Forcing students to revise two, three, or more times is of little value, once they feel they've nothing more to say, or think their meaning is reasonably clear. But if writers are adding new information, changing their meaning, or altering form, they may want additional responses to the new vision. In some cases, it will make sense to suggest a second version, especially in the case of complicated writing such as a research paper. Up to this point the process will be the same as for an original draft, only this time the writer will have noted the changes from the first draft. As many versions as the writer has stamina for are possible, but eventually some agreement is reached between the responder and the writer and the piece is now ready for editing.

Editing

In an imporant piece of research into the composing process, Sondra Perl (1978) discovered the effects of premature attention to form. Perl studied several adult students at a community college in New York who were considered "basic writers," having never learned to write successfully during their previous school experience. Before they could continue with their college studies, they had to complete a composition course. She asked them to compose aloud and recorded what they said while they were writing. What she discovered was astounding: in all cases, the writers were unable to produce more than three or four words before they began to worry about whether they'd spelled or punctuated correctly, or used the appropriate verb form.

The most important consequence of their anxiety about correctness was the effect it had on their thought processes and their ability to create meaning. Because they were so quickly stymied, they were rarely able to get a clear thought across. By ceasing to write in order to work on a surface feature problem, the writers lost their train of thought, forgot what they'd originally intended to say, and invariably needed to start over again to attempt to recapture their original meaning. The result was that very little text was ever produced, and what did finally emerge was so garbled and choppy as to be almost incomprehensible.

For more than 70 years, studies have concluded that the teaching and learning of grammar, punctuation, and usage have no direct effect on improving a student's writing. Now, recent studies like Perl's show us why the teaching and learning of grammar before a writer's fluency has been developed can have such a disastrous effect on writing. Yet we know that correctness is important, and that we're judged by it. What solutions can we find to deal with this disparity, to help students write both fluently and with correct form?

It should be clear that our first task as writing teachers is to encourage students to write as often as possible. To accomplish this we must heed Perl's results: we cannot worry about conventions before students have had the freedom to concentrate solely on meaning. Even very young children begin to write to communicate meaning, although their mastery of conventions may be non-existent. Yet soon they recognize, partly in conjunction with reading, that for people to understand them, they must master certain conventions. For older students who have not learned this lesson, the teacher's task is to link the writer's control of mechanics to her ability to create a formally finished text. A student must recognize that the rules of syntax, punctuation and spelling are essential to communicating ideas, not that they are in themselves the arbitrary subject matter of English classes.

Judgment is really the issue here. For some inexplicable reason, Amercans have become obsessed with spelling. This has led us to use surface features like spelling not only to judge a writer's ability but further to judge her intelligence and even her moral character. If the writer has misspelled a word, our fuzzy logic tells us, obviously she's not too smart, or at best is lazy and uncaring about her writing and possibly about the rest of herself as well. Because readers make such judgments about the writer on the basis of surface mechanics, the merits of the actual message can escape notice. However unfortunate this phenomenon may be, we must communicate its import to our students. Unless they're prepared to clean up their act, many readers will never bother to seek their meanings, obscured as they are by too many surface blemishes.

The best way to get students genuinely concerned about editing is to provide a variety of audiences for their writing. If students know that you will not be their sole audience, that other students—peers as well as older and younger students—or the principal, the school board, the mayor, or a company president will also be reading their writing, they will begin to see that if they want to make a good (i.e., intelligent and moral) impression, they'd better make sure that what they've written is as correct in its form as it is in its message.

Students should learn correctness in a meaningful context. When students edit each other's work there is valid reason for them to learn, for example, where commas go, or what a sentence is, because they'll actually be employing these skills to help fellow students. If students are required to correct each other's writing, they will themselves begin to heed mechanics, spelling and grammar. Along with this they must be involved in a rich and varied reading program wherein they can develop an "ear" for good writing.

Dan Kirby and Tom Liner (1981) make an excellent proposal for helping students edit: the editorial board. The term itself connotes a real world job. Kirby and Liner suggest that a group of three to four students who have the best editorial skills in the class should be the first members chosen for the board. These students would be responsible for the spelling, punctuation and grammar of each final piece of writing produced in class. When a student is finished with a piece, but before it is submitted for evaluation, the editorial board checks it for surface errors.

Because more than one student is responsible for editing, it's likely that some disagreements will arise. But one of the best ways to learn a rule of grammar is to defend it in a live situation. The student who disagrees will have to know why. The teacher should be available for consultation, but the greatest responsibility will lie with the editorial board.

Once students get used to this process, the board's membership can rotate. This will enable every student to play the role of editor, not just the good spellers or experts on participle danglings. The more experienced editors can help the less experienced by teaching them during their editing job. As members of the editorial board, students will actually use what they have learned.

Publishing

A "published" piece of writing is simply one that the student feels ready to deliver to the public or to the teacher. Although not every piece that achieves this readiness will ever be published formally, there are a number of ways that student work can go public. These range from inclusion in student or community publications (newspapers, magazines, "shoppers") to creating class magazines, classroom libraries of student work, bound books for the school library, and even posting work in the classroom or around the school. Sending a letter to a public official or a company, drafting a petition, writing out an accident report also qualify as publication.

The main reason for using the term *publication* to denote the process of producing a public version of a text is to explicitly recognize the importance of developing the sense of pride in craft as part of the process of learning to write. No one will work hard at a task unless it's toward a worthwhile goal. Practice doesn't happen for the sake of practice; some greater end must be present. Writers who get published or want to are much more likely to put in the necessary effort at revising and editing to make the final product live up to its initial intentions. And while products alone are not our exclusive focus of energy, the whole aim of the composing process is to produce the best possible, hence publishable, product.

WRITING TO LEARN

1. From your journal, your work or your daily life, choose some problem or idea that you would like to explore more through writing. Write a *first* draft on this topic. Make sure this piece of writing responds to a real problem and can be addressed to a real audience. You might, for instance, write a proposal for a new course or unit with supporting rationale, a letter to an editor about a community problem, a definition of your own position on an issue that concerns you. Keep it relatively brief. The idea is to experiment. Be tentative and messy, not exhaustive and neat.
2. Reflect on and write down the steps you went through in writing your draft. Did you do it all in one sitting? What did you do before you actually started to write? How many changes did you make as you went along? What kinds? Why did you make them?
3. Try writing a short paragraph on an idea that interests you and monitor the stream of thoughts in your head as they occur. (You could even try talking

into a tape recorder—composing aloud—as you write.) Can you see a back and forth pattern in your composing process?

4. Brainstorm a list of activites for your students that might lead to writing. Alongside each activity, write a brief description of what kind of writing could occur out of this activity and a short explanation of why such writing would be the most appropriate.
5. Revise either the piece of writing you did in Task 1 or Task 3. List the reasons for each revision. List the types of revisions you made (i.e., paragraph changes, addition of new material, deletions). When you shared your draft, what comments, questions led to your revisions? How different are your two papers? How often did you consider audience and purpose? What were most of your revisions like? What cues did you respond to in making the changes: spelling? sentence structure? organization? logic?
6. Edit the piece of writing you revised in Task 5. What were the most common problems? How did you solve them? (Did you go to a dictionary for spelling, for example?)
7. Compare the steps you went through to write your final "publishable" piece of writing with the composing process model presented in this chapter. What are the similarities? The differences? How did you create meaning in your writing? How many times did you return to an earlier part of the paper before you proceeded to write more? When did you go back?

4

Writing from a Developmental Perspective

Writing and reading abilities can develop naturally from the language system that has earlier been mastered for speaking and listening, but more often than not they don't. This chapter will explore both how they can and why they usually don't by charting some of the relations among the spoken and written language systems, examining the characteristics of beginning writers, maturing writers, and those for whom writing hasn't come easily, and explaining the role of instruction in facilitating the growth of writing ability. The basic premise of this chapter is that while learning to write is never a simple process, it can be less traumatic and more successful when approached developmentally than has traditionally been the case when it has been approached analytically.

The Development of Language

We're not born with a full-fledged ability to converse with our parents, but we do have an innate capacity to acquire language. All non-deaf children develop the ability to speak and understand the language being spoken around them as naturally as they learn to walk, focus their eyes binocularly, and grasp and manipulate objects with their hands. Although there's considable controversy about the relative importance of nature and nurture in the development of language, it seems clear that humans are uniquely capable of developing one, and that to do so they need an interactive relationship with other speakers.

The need for this interactive relation points to one of our key roles as parents and teachers, since it is this aspect of language development we can influence. The quality of that interaction makes for the individual differences we see among language users. Our consciousness of differences sometimes leads us to fail to recognize that the similarities are even more striking. By the time he comes to school, every non-deaf child has mastered a language system which enables him to produce and understand a potentially infinite number of sentences following the "rules" of a highly complex "grammar." The fact that some people become more able language users than others should not obscure the magnitude of this common achievement.

Many Grammars

We put *rules* and *grammar* in quotes above to emphasize that such rules and such a grammar operate completely out of the conscious awareness of the speaker-hearer. English-speaking children learn to ask yes-no questions by inverting the subject with the first element of the auxiliary as in:

Is the cake ready to eat?

French-speaking children learn to ask similar questions by saying:

Est-ce que le gateau est prêt à manger?

But five-year-olds in either culture do so completely without consciously following any rules.

Part of the confusion surrounding such terms as *grammar* and *rule* results from the fact that linguists use the terms with a systematic ambiguity. When one says that a normal five-year-old has mastered the grammar of his language, it's something akin to saying that he had learned to run; that is, he controls a system without being conscious of the system itself. Language researchers attempt to describe the system that underlies his capacity to talk, and part of the confusion ensues because these descriptions are also spoken of as grammars.

No one actually gets very confused about the differences between the biologically and psychologically realized grammar (Grammar I) that enables us to talk, and the linguist's more or less successful attempts to build a model of it (Grammar II). These grammars are clearly distinct from one another. The problem arises when teachers operate on the mistaken notion that one must know the rules of the second sort of grammar to speak and listen or, particularly, to read and write. There is, potentially, some role for Grammar II knowledge in some aspects of the writing process, but it's absurd to maintain that such knowledge is a prerequisite to using the language system. It's possible to become a fully competent speaker, listener, reader *and* writer without ever having heard terms like *noun* or *relative clause,* much less being able to identify or define them.

Some teachers have argued that while it's true that students can produce relative clauses without knowing it, they need to be able to identify and define such beasts in order to have a vocabulary to talk with their teacher about their errors. In fact, it's rarely the case that such a vocabulary is used except in a few areas like those of subject-verb agreement or pronoun case and reference problems. And even these can be more appropriately discussed (and better learned) if they are attended to as *clarity* issues rather than *correctness* problems. If such terms are needed, they can be presented better in the context of the writer's meaning-shaping process than in isolated drills and exercises.

The situation is made even worse by the existence of still a third sort of grammar (Grammar III) which is essentially *prescriptive* in orientation. Such grammars attempt not to characterize or describe what people do when they speak and listen, but to legislate or prescribe what they ought to do. "Rules" like "Never split an infinitive," "Don't end a sentence with a preposition," or "Use *It is I* instead of *It's me*," are intended to guide the writer (and to some extent the speaker) toward what such grammarians believe to be a higher standard of writing and speech.

When such rules are imposed as guidelines for stylistic choices based on aesthetic preferences and traditions of standard usage, they can have some value in developing the "ear" for the written language so essential to mature writing. Such phenomena cannot be understood, however, out of the context of choices that a writer actually makes while drafting and revising. They are *not* the basics of writing instruction or its necessary prerequisites. Research study after research study has shown that knowledge of prescriptive grammar and usage rules does *not* transfer to writing ability.

The Persistence of Grammar Teaching

Grammar continues to be taught, not only because of a conceptual confusion among types and purposes of grammars, but because of the mistaken belief that grammatical choices in writing ought to be a matter of conscious control. Ironically, it's precisely this view that causes many of the most severe writing problems, as we'll see when we look at basic writers. Even fluent writers would become pen-tied if they had to be conscious of using an adverb clause or a predicate nominative while they were composing. Linguists can parse or analyze most sentences *after* they have been produced, but to stop and worry about the structure of the sentence they're producing would make them literally unable to produce it.

This analysis procedure persists in part because teachers confronted by grammatically mangled texts identify the errors analytically. They then seem to assume that better texts will be produced if students can learn to analyze language consciously and use this analytical skill to produce error-free texts. By focusing exclusively on products, instead of on the process of composing, they foreshorten the developing writer's view of his task so that he comes to believe that error-free texts are the goal of writing and that such texts can be produced the first time one writes.

On a more general level, such teaching persists because mastery of writing is seen as different from mastery of speaking. If the natural process of learning to speak and listen is considered at all, it's dismissed precisely because it *is* natural and therefore doesn't require conscious teaching or learning. Since people have traditionally learned to read and write in school, and since not everybody seems to master these skills, it has been assumed that they require explicit instruction.

The evidence is not all in—the processes of learning to read and write are matters of intensive current study—but what we know doesn't confirm traditional wisdom. There are many examples of children who learn to read and write in ways that seem far more analogous to how they learned to talk. They do need exposure to the written language and a purposeful context for wanting to make meaning from their reading and writing, but they require little explicit instruction. To move their own invented spelling systems closer to conventional usage requires some instruction or at least shared connection-making in the form of reader feedback, but many of our cherished assumptions about the role of teaching in initial writing and reading are just plain wrong.

As in the learning of the spoken language, what learners seem to need above all is an interactive environment where meaning-making is the primary end. Other characteristics of such an environment are the recognition that "errors" can signify learning, not ignorance; that they are errors only because the learning has not yet reached adult standards. No one would criticize a toddler for producing "dada" instead of "daddy" or fail to recognize that "dada" represented learning. In helping children grow as writers we must stop insisting on error avoidance and work instead on moving toward mastery through practice, constructive feedback, and a focus on meaning rather than form.

KAREN GREENBERG Teachers honestly believe, especially English teachers, that their good writers are good because they learned their grammar. There's a 2000-year-old tradition of grammar being good for the mind—it provides training in logic—and that somehow if you apply rules to sentences, sentences will get better. So, I think, it's a very honest misconception. Also, teachers have the textbooks and they're comfortable with them. They get social reinforcement. They read critics like John Simon, who talk about protecting the English language from decay, and they think they're doing their part. And, finally, I think that teachers really believe that if students knew their grammar better they would write better.

Other factors contributing to a continuation of grammar teaching include the general climate of instruction built upon a behaviorist model which sees complex learning as the chaining together of simpler bits. Words are thought to be composed entirely of separable parts which can be learned independently. A good example of this is the phonics approach to reading instruction which focuses first on letter-sound correspondences and next on how they combine into words. This approach tends to make learners equate reading with word calling; and by failing to recognize the centrality of meaning making as the end of reading, it has produced a generation of "remedial" readers.

Such approaches have been thoroughly discounted by students of language acquisition and reading for some time (see, for example, Chomsky, 1959, Goodman, 1969, and Smith, 1973), but they still persist in many classrooms. Unfortunately, attempts to replace such analytic/bottom-up approaches have been hampered by the continued use of tests which judge analytic skills to be a measure of reading and writing ability. As more and more states adopt such tests to ensure accountability, a well-intended desire to promote improvement in reading and writing ends up sabotaging the entire effort.

Learning to Mean with the Written Language

In a home environment where reading and writing are valued and natural, many children begin to read or write before they come to school. While such activity is relatively rare, it does suggest certain characteristics which should be part of the early school environment. There must be a high regard for the written language as a source of meaning and pleasure for each child. This is another way of saying that *fluency* is the initial goal of writing instruction, but more important it's a claim that every other aspect of developing writing abilities is subordinate to meaning making.

A child's first spoken words are intended to be meaningful, and so are his first efforts at writing. They may not be successful at communicating their meaning (as, for example, with a child who merely scribbles or writes only consonants). Indeed, children's initial oral productions often partially misfire when they aren't understood, or when their mothers can understand them long before anyone else can. Anne Dyson's study (1981) of children's initial writing strategies suggests an interesting parallel here in that one of her subjects expressed a clear belief that even though he couldn't interpret his own scribbles, he was sure his mother would be able to.

The beginning reader and writer must recognize that the squiggles on paper are another way of representing the same things that he is saying and hearing. He must further learn to understand that in reading the text never changes, and that in writing there's a conventional way of representing language. Reading is learned primarily through repeated oral comprehension of the same text, long before a child can read, as any parent knows who has tried to condense or skip parts of a familiar story in an attempt to speed a child off to bed. The child's objections are the beginning of reading ability. Writing is learned when the child discovers that others cannot interpret his representational system and moves to make it more conventional. This last point reveals that *clarity* and *correctness* play at least a role in the beginning stages of writing.

The Development of Writing Abilities and the Writing Process

Although children come to school with a highly developed oral language system and some preliminary mastery of the written system, both sets of abilities continue to develop throughout the school years. Vocabularly is continually added to the child's repertoire, and each new word brings with it a complex set of constraints on how and when the word should be used. Similarly, increasing use of the written language demands the mastery of those constructions which are more characteristic of writing than talk, including passives, sentences with introductory subordinate clauses, and various kinds of parallel constructions. Children who read and write increasingly complex texts find the need for and develop the ability to use richer and richer linguistic options.

The growth of writing abilities and the writing process are interactive in that both are focused on meaning. One aspect or another of either may have prominence at a given time, but since all parts of each must interact to promote growth or to produce a text, no one aspect can be considered independently. Linguists have observed that even the first words children speak are meant to be complete and meaningful utterances and that these single words have sentence-like properties of meaning. The same is true with early writing, whether the texts are labels, names, scribbles or strings of consonants representing the initial sound of each word of a sentence.

Our choice of *fluency* as the aspect of writing development to be emphasized first is based on the recognition that meaning is every writer's first goal and that focusing on fluency will be the best way of relating the child's emerging control of the written language to his more fully developed mastery of the oral system. Part of what this means in practice is that children should be encouraged from the start to produce complete and meaningful texts, not to copy or fill in the blanks in someone else's text. Traditional, exercise-based, analytical approaches to teaching writing have tried to help children overcome their fears of writing by such self-limiting strategies. By emphasizing form at the expense of meaning, however, they have had an opposite effect and have also made writing seem purposeless. Considering fluency as the growing mastery of the means of expressing one's own meaning on paper can help children feel confident that they can control the process even if they have some difficulties, and that it will be worth the struggle.

Emphasizing fluency first doesn't mean neglecting either clarity or correctness even at the start. Rather than seeing these as independent stages of development, it's probably more accurate to characterize them as interacting aspects of writing ability through which writers cycle over and over as they mature. Like the process of writing a particular text, the process of growing in confidence and competence as a writer is not a smooth, linear progression. Each new writing project presents new challenges, and writers who have the capacity to produce texts fluently in one genre may be quite dysfluent in another.

This interaction can be seen in every text. Matt S., a second grader, writes:

I went to the hospidl wn I was young
I had the ammonia

Matt is expressing his intentions here in a meaningful way. Even though he has some problems with correctness, his reader will not be confused. He probably could be more fluent in the sense of telling us what is was like in the hospital, which would also make us better able to be clear about what the experience meant to him. By placing the initial emphasis on fluency, however, we establish that we're interested in his experience and that he doesn't need to worry *now* about the conventions of written English as he struggles to express himself more fully. Calling him to account for misspellings is more likely to retard rather than enhance his development, since to do so might encourage him to avoid using words he can't spell.

He can learn that as he attempts to express himself more fluently, he will also become clearer to his readers. Part of the interaction of fluency and clarity is based on the recognition that texts are changeable even after they have been written the first time. Revision based on rethinking, reviewing, and reinventing is a characteristic of both fluency—to better express one's intentions—and clarity—to better communicate to a reader. Too many writers have learned that texts should be complete upon first expression, perhaps because speech must be, or perhaps because they never see anyone else's first attempts. Integrating our attempts to develop student writing abilities with an understanding of the interactive nature of the processes of writing will help us see that both processes will develop best if they are subordinated to a concern for meaning-making.

The Characteristics of Beginning Writers

It has long been recognized that young children are egocentric in the Piagetian sense of thinking that their view of the world is *the* view. As it affects their beginning writing, this egocentrism is both a strength and a weakness. It can be an asset to developing fluency since many young writers (like many young talkers) are convinced the world will be interested in their stories. A visitor arriving in Cheryl Miceli's classroom in Paradise Valley, Arizona is immediately surrounded by children eager to read him their essay or poem or play. And the intensity which students of Margaret Grant's class in Missoula, Montana devote to journal writing shows the pleasure that students can get from the sheer act of making meaning—of shaping at the point of utterance—in texts which are primarily self-addressed although they are sometimes shared with teacher and class.

Children love to tell stories, but the stories they tell, at least initially, are—and should be—personal. They are intimately involved with the teller's experience and are one of the ways the teller makes meaning out of that experience. Lisa Ann Jarvi's poignant story about the death of her dog and its antidote in the playful antics of her cat was originally written as a journal entry and later shared with the class:

> I used to have a dog Brandy but she got hit by a truck and stayed alive until we got to the vets. And she was still alive but the next morning she died. I was really sad. She meant a lot to me. I taught her almost everything she knew. I taught her to sit, beg and I taught her to walk on a leash. Then I taught her to shake, roll over and she always used to have the saddest eyes. When she would sit by the dinner table she would look at everybody and somebody would give her a scrap of food. But whenever she did that she would sit by me and she would wrinkle her forehead when she did her sad trick with her eyes. I really miss her a lot. "Brandy come home," I said. And I cried and cried and cried. And I always think about her whenever I talk about her I get tears in my eyes. I really miss her a lot.
>
> I have a cat Fritz. He is really neat. He sort of talks to you. He always sleeps with me. And when he jumps up on my bed he will meow, like he says, "Hi, Lisa. How are you today?" And I always said "meow" back to him. And we would keep talking. And in the morning I wouldn't be able to get up. He would lay there on my stomach and never get up. But finally I get up and I get ready for school, which usually takes a long time because I am always tired. But I gradually get done. Then I go out and eat breakfast, but he is always right there rubbing on my leg gripping because he wants some food. So I have to interrupt my breakfast and feed him. He does it all the time. Every morning he does that but I don't get mad because I think it's fun to stay in bed half the morning.

Margaret Grant's sensitive response to Lisa about the story's meaning shows how personal writing can be a way of meaning making and, in this case, of working through a painful experience:

> Thank you. I noticed something. You started that March 31, during general writing time; then you worked on it on the second of April. You came back to it on the 9th of April. And I suspect that in the meantime you were writing some other things, but you kept coming back to your story. I think that's a great way to do it. Stories don't have to be written in one day. They don't all have to be finished all the same time. Sometimes it's kind of nice to let ideas like this one, which is such a good one, kind of cook in our heads for a while. When we're in the mood we can come back to them again.
>
> Your story is very special to me because the last part is very funny and very happy because it tells how much you love your crazy cat. 'Cause the first part does something entirely different. It tells those really hard feelings when you lost your dog and what the dog meant to you. And that's one of the advantages to having a journal.

Such storytelling can also give free play to the imagination:

Betsy and the Cat

I have a dog. Her name is Betsy. One day there was a scratch at the door. It wasn't Betsy because she was already inside. It was a cat. Now this wasn't an ordinary cat. This cat was all colors. I went to the door and let him in and fed him. This was no easy task. Why? Because the cat was very picky about his food and all he liked was water and toast with jelly. He ate it greedily. Now comes the strange part. Betsy started chasing him, but instead of running, wings came out of his back and he rose into the air. Betsy was frantic. We laughed at Betsy, but we hadn't forgotten about the cat. He was flying around the room and was about to fly through the door. Betsy ran after him but it was too late. The cat had already disappeared through the door. Betsy ran to the door. We let her out. The cat was no where in sight.

Once I thought I saw the rainbow cat but it was only a colored piece of cloth. I sighed. Ummmm. Suddenly Betsy started to bark like mad. We said, "it must be the cat." "The cat," someone said. "I am the cat," the cat said. "You will never catch me. If you do I will give you any wish you wish. But if you don't I will go where I like and don't try to stop me. If you do try, I will cast a spell on you all, especially the dog. I will come back often to check on you," the cat said. "But, but why?" I asked. "Because I will figure out if I can stay if you are nice enough for me to tolerate you," said the cat.

Betsy started chasing after him. He flew on to the antenna. Betsy ran around the house a few times and then she found a patch of clover and settled down to watch the cat. The cat didn't mind as long as Betsy stayed down. "When are you going to come down," I asked. "Not for a long time," said the cat. "Well, we might as well go to sleep now," said Dad. "But somebody has to secretly guard the house so nobody can catch the cat," he whispered. "I will," I said. "O.K.," he said. We went to sleep but Betsy really started chasing the cat. When we awoke the next morning we were listening for a scratch on the door from Betsy. We didn't hear one. I was worried about Betsy. We went outside to look for her but could not find her anywhere.

Meanwhile Betsy had run a mile now after the cat. The cat had flown into the cave and hid from Betsy. Betsy was tired from running so far, but she found the cave and the cat flew through a hole in the roof. Betsy started running after her. She at last picked up speed. She raced ahead of the cat looking back occasionally at the cat. The cat slowed down for a landing. At once Betsy hid where she knew the cat would land. The cat said, "Land there," and Betsy had him trapped. The cat moaned and said, "O.K. what's your wish?" Betsy said, "I wish that I could have people fooled all the time," "O.K.," said the cat. "You have your wish now."

The End

Molly Carmody was playing with language in her journal entry as well as with reality, and both kinds of expression are part of the process of building her capacity to understand her world, her mind, and the other people in it. Her line, "Once I thought I saw the rainbow cat, but it was only a colored piece of cloth," is a powerful example of the way children use language to explore the boundaries of reality and to celebrate the powers of imagination. In emphasizing the strengths that egocentrism and personal writing bring to the emerging writer we're not ignoring the weaknesses, chiefly the writer's conviction that his readers share his inner world, hear his inner voice, and are as ready and able to comprehend the text as he is. While many beginning writers recognize that they have problems with the conventions of the written language, they're usually far less aware of problems of clarity. To a degree this is a problem for all writers, but this lack of a sense of audience is most characteristic of beginners.

Donald Graves and his colleagues, in particular Lucy Calkins, have shown that early on children can become aware of clarity, style, and general effectiveness. To do so they seem to need several things. First, and most basic, is a caring reader to provide supportive feedback. They need to know what meaning they're making and learn to recognize mismatches between intended and received meanings. Second, they need to learn that their drafts can be changed. As Lucy Calkins puts it, "They need to learn to make it messy before they learn to make it neat again."

Calkins illustrates this with the story of a young boy who had drawn a picture of a dinosaur and captioned it with the statement: "Brontosaurus may have stayed in groups." His teacher then asked him: "Why did Brontosaurus stay in groups?" He replied, "To protect the young, of course." He knew the information; the problem was that he assumed his readers did too—egocentrism in action. She then said, "Don't you think you should add that in?" He said: "I guess so, but there's no room." Then, quite reluctantly, he re-examined his paper and discovered room for it in the upper-right corner. He was still reluctant to change his text because he knew books didn't look like that (correctness in action) and because he was afraid people couldn't follow his thought. He finally compromised with an arrow—first a small one, then a longer one—which made his picture/caption more messy, but which more fully and clearly expressed *his* meaning.

LUCY CALKINS First graders often don't begin to know what they're going to write about until they actually sit down with paper in front of them. Until they begin to draw they don't have any idea what it is they're going to write about. Later in first grade as they begin to draw profiles, more action can be put into their pictures. This action leads to a story happening in the picture. When you get action into the drawing, it often means that the narratives, the stories, get action into them. Early on, when children write, their books look like a list or a description, but there's not a real action sequence—one thing happening, then the next and then the next.

They might begin writing in response to what a teacher is saying: "I know you don't know all the sounds. I know you don't know all your letters. But that's O.K. because I know you've got something worth saying—a message—and all I want you to do is to listen and put down whatever sounds you hear." The student will draw a picture, sound out the words of what it is and write that down. The student might bring the drawing and writing up to the teacher. If the teacher is a good one, she'll know to take the child's print seriously and she'll say: "Please point to each word as you read it." So the student is drawn back to her own letters. The teacher has said they matter to her, remember. The student then reads what she has written, which is usually only the initial consonants, but which, for the student, represent whole words and sentences.

Once children know that texts can be changed, they can be encouraged to make changes. If practice in revision is desirable, with beginners it's probably better to concentrate on beginnings and endings or with additions rather than on the whole story. One factor militating against having young children revise is that the sheer mechanical difficulty of writing makes rewriting painful and may bring more discouragement than learning. Furthermore, if fluency is the primary goal at this stage, incorporating the insights gained from considering the possible revision of Story A into the production of a new story B may be more beneficial and more fun.

Introducing young children to writing should be done as much as possible in the context of their own lives so that writing becomes as natural and normal a means of expression as talking already is. The first effort should be to encourage children to write regularly—an hour a day is hardly too much—

in a workshop atmosphere where sharing is natural and expected. They should write about what they know—to help make sense of it and share it—and they should write about that they are learning, to help make connections between what they already know and what they are discovering.

Growing Mature Writers

To help maturing writers develop their capacities for clarity and recognize the actual rather than the "official" value of correctness, the key ingredient is still meaning. Once children learn that writing can signify and express meaning, they should next become concerned with whether or not their readers are receiving what they're sending. Although all writers retain some of the egocentric belief that people will understand them, mature writers recognize that to be understood, they must have a sense of who their reading audience is.

Mature writers, like mature people, come in all shapes and sizes, so it's impossible to be very precise about any necessary characteristics. That said, three special traits can be seen as benchmarks. The most important is probably *flexibility*. A mature writer is one who usually succeeds in writing with a sufficient variety of styles to make the text appropriate for its intended purpose and audience. Second, mature writers exhibit *confidence.* Such writers may still be apprehensive about beginning a writing task and even occasionally run into a mild case of writer's block, but in general they have confidence in their abilities. The third is a sense of their own *voice* as writers. This is related to confidence and flexibility, but what it means, additionally, is a willingness to sound like an individual writing to other individuals. All of these characteristics taken together are essentially *matured fluency.*

Recognizing that a writer's development takes time and practice is particularly crucial because it emphasizes that writers are made not born, and that any given writing task will not miraculously produce right results. We're dealing with a learning process which we continue to master throughout our lives. Pedagogically this implies the need for a long-term view of how writing develops throughout the curriculum from kindergarten through at least freshman year of college. This process involves a continual building on the oral language system that is developing throughout this period, but for mature talkers to become mature writers, the special demands of the written language and its voices must be mastered as well.

This is sometimes difficult for young writers. As developing language users they have had extensive practice with the oral language system and have thereby learned to master the logic of conversation. Unfortunately, the rules of conversation give poor guidance to the writer. The give-and-take nature of talk makes brevity a virtue and requires each participant to do a substantial amount of filling in to make sense of the interchange. In conversation there is always the option of saying, "I don't follow that," or "How does that relate?" In reading one doesn't have the writer available, so the burden of explicitness is greater.

Something like a failure to be explicit or to fill in the gaps seems to be going on in the following paper. As you read it try to determine what its strengths and weaknesses are:

> Today is the "Age of Computers." Computers are being used by almost everyone today. I think people are depending too much on computers these days. People can do the same things computers can do, but the computer does them much faster. Computers are taking jobs away from people because it is cheaper to run a computer than to pay somebody. I personally find computers difficult to use and I don't like to use them. I'm not totally against the use of computers, though. Computers have made life easier for man. I think computers should be used for hard problems, and not all problems.

Although the writer—a 17-year-old boy with limited writing experience—isn't completely without literacy skills, the paper just doesn't work as written discourse. Some cohesion exists; the word *computer* is used throughout, although stylistically its appearance is excessive, since there are virtually no transitional elements. But the argument is hard to determine; the logical connections among the various statements are missing. We have a vague sense of the writer's dissatisfaction with creeping computerism and his apprehension about his own interaction with computers, but there's little here that's clear and coherent communication of ideas on paper.

There's another way of looking at this paper, however, and that is as a written-down version of a conversation. What do you make of it when you read it arranged as an internal dialogue?

> A: Today is the "Age of Computers." Computers are being used by almost everyone today.
> B: I think people are depending too much on computers today.
> A: People can do the same things computers can do, but the computer does it much faster.
> B: Computers are taking jobs away from people because it is cheaper to run a computer than to pay somebody.
> A: I personally find computers difficult to use, and I don't like to use them.
> B. I'm not totally against the use of computers, though. Computers have made life easier for man.
> A. I think computers should be used for hard problems, and not all problems.

Such a layout is a bit artificial, but seeing it this way provides a shift in perspective. One can easily imagine an inexperienced writer having an internal conversation with very similar properties. What we need to help ourselves and our students see is why a logical internal dialogue isn't the same as a logical paper.

Even without extensive additions, this paper would work better as a written text if the elements were combined differently and the first sentence used as a title.

> *Today is the "Age of Computers"*
> Computers are being used by almost everyone today because the computer does things much faster than people can, even though people can do the same things. This has had two unfortunate effects: computers are taking jobs away from people because it is cheaper to run a computer than to pay somebody, and people are depending too much on computers.
>
> I'm not totally against the use of computers. Even though I personally find computers difficult to use and I don't like to use them, computers have made life easier for man. The best solution, I think, would be to use computers for hard problems, but not for all problems.

While this version is far from being a fully adequate argument, it does have more of the logic of the written language and is less like conversation. The addition of transitional elements and some minor reordering has made it move toward writing and away from speech. Fleshing out the arguments, deciding which can be supported and which depend only on his personal fears, and adding more information could help the writer still further. Even the personal fear elements can be made more general if the writer can show that most people find computers threatening.

Maturing writers should be encouraged to use internal dialogues to help them shape opinions and build arguments, but they must also learn not to stop there. Readers need more explicit guidance and more extensive presentations of the *whys* of our ideas, and the mature writer has a clear sense of what his audience first needs to understand his position and then to be convinced by it.

The key to fostering such developments in the classroom is to create a community of writers and readers who are supportive of and interested in each other's work. For such a workshop atmosphere to happen, the central figure remains the teacher, who must become the model writer/reader for the class. One of the easiest ways to help students learn to value and carry out extensive revisions is to have them do so in imitation of their teacher. And, more generally, for the teachers to show their own vulnerability and imperfections to their students helps create the kind of atmosphere where experimentation and growth can happen.

Teachers must write alongside their students. This may mean writing the same assignments or it may mean writing something for which the teacher has his own purpose and audience: a curriculum proposal, a memo to the school board, or even a lesson plan. It must mean sharing work in progress with the class so that they can see the beginning and middle steps of the evolving text. Teachers should also talk with their class about their own composing processes and about problems they may be having with writing. Seeing an "expert" adult have trouble and need revision and reader feedback can help provide one path to the trustful atmosphere necessary for a writing workshop to work.

Too often student writers choose the safest path because they're afraid to fail. And yet, when one tries a new form or technique, or attempts to reach a new audience, initial failures are likely. Inexperienced writers, for example, will frequently avoid using a new word which would be apt and choose instead the one they know how to spell. Even more failure-ridden is the great secondary school leap from narration to exposition. Narration has its roots in personal experience, which makes it a relatively comfortable form. It can also be a natural basis for the generalizing needed for essay writing. Stories, after all, must have a point, even, as fables, a moral. And the point of stories is often the first sort of generalization made by maturing writers. The transition to more abstract generalizing isn't always a smooth one, but failures which result from trying out new approaches are to be lauded.

An issue related to expecting and even welcoming failures is how to establish criteria for judging writing. Such criteria must be understood by our students. For writers to recognize either the need for or the reality of improvement, they must be able to distinguish bad from good.

In developing criteria we shouldn't be put off by the fact that we're not dealing with objectively measurable phenomena. The "objective" things we can measure, such as the average length of clauses or T-units, the number of misspellings per thousand words, are very countable, but they don't measure quality in writing. What do seem to work are subjective consensus measures. They work because quality in writing is by definition intersubjective. That is, whether or not a piece of writing succeeds is determined jointly by the writer and his readers. Different readers may disagree somewhat but through reading, sharing and comparing, broad consensus criteria can be established. In a writing workshop atmosphere, such criteria evolve informally and quite naturally, but it's also important to make them explicit so that student writers can learn to judge their own and others' efforts constructively.

Writers can develop their own capacities as assessors of and talkers about writing by developing questions to ask about their texts. The following serve as examples, but the process will work best if students develop their own with teacher guidance.

- Does my draft say everything I wanted to say?
- Did I leave out anything important?
- Have I anticipated what my readers know and don't know?
- Does it have a clear and interesting beginning? (Why should anyone read Sentence 2 after Sentence 1?)
- Do the parts relate clearly to each other? (Can a reader follow me from sentence to sentence? From paragraph to paragraph?)
- Is there anything that could be eliminated? (Are all the parts needed?)
- How will my reader react? (Will he be convinced? interested? bored?)
- Is there a satisfying ending?
- Do I sound the way I want to sound?
- Have I left in any errors in spelling, punctuation, agreement, etc.?

Having students consider such questions before they judge a text to be finished will go a long way toward developing mature capacities for fluency, clarity, and correctness as well as the ability to use all aspects of the composing process. Mature writers avoid premature closure of their writing process, and to nurture more mature writers in our classrooms, we must give them time, response and support.

When Things Go Wrong: Basic Writers

Although there have been periodic bouts of public concern and professional breast-beating about our failures to teach everyone to write, the current perception of a "writing crisis" is more widespread and enduring than its predecessors. With the opening up of many college and community college programs to "non-traditional" students in the late sixties and early seventies, college writing instructors found themselves confronting record numbers of students whose written work didn't conform to their expectations. These students weren't really like the bonehead English students of earlier generations who tended to be from high schools that hadn't provided much writing practice or who just hadn't worked very hard; they were, instead, minority students—many of them black—and second language speakers—many of them Hispanic—and adult returnees to an educational system where they'd failed the first time around.

Most college composition programs responded with "remedial" courses—usually non-credit. These had the advantage of keeping "real" freshman English pure, while enabling colleges to hire special teachers to do the dirty work which the regular faculty eschewed. That this special faculty could be segregated in non-tenure track positions also helped to insulate the English department—and the college as a whole—from confronting the problems.

Although there are still plenty of colleges which haven't solved these problems, in the last decade we've seen some encouraging developments. The most important has been that the special teachers didn't just dole out remediation. Instead they picked up the challenge of trying to understand who these writers were, what their writing was like, where it came from, how it was created, and what could be done to change it. Unsatisfied with conventional answers and solutions, some did their own research and began developing a clearer picture of basic writers and a more effective pedagogy for dealing with their problems.

The driving force behind many of these developments was Mina Shaughnessy of New York's City College, whose *Errors and Expectations* was published in 1977. The book presented a series of challenges to the profession to change our perceptions of these students and their problems. Shaughnessy coined the term "basic" to characterize these writers in an attempt to find a better, more descriptive label for a set of phenomena which we're still trying to understand.

The simplistic view that basic writers are students who "don't know how to write" will no longer stand scrutiny. Particularly crucial is the difference between beginning writers who really don't know how to write because they're just starting to learn, and basic writers who've had many years of "writing instruction" but who are still producing mangled texts. In many instances the problem of basic writers is more the result of knowledge, however incomplete or poorly applied, than of ignorance.

The most distinctive characteristic of basic writers is that they've somehow fallen behind. They aren't performing well as writers. And they know it. So they come to writing with all kinds of failure-based fears and anxieties. As noted earlier, the bottom-up teaching approach to writing has created many fearful writers, but those we're calling "basic" are the most fearful of all. Confronted with texts like that of Louella, below, most writing teachers would have been overwhelmed by the errors it contains and puzzled by how it came into being (Perl, 1978):

> I believe that the problem of New York City is being threatened because New York is suppose to be one of the hottest spot in the Nation because of the entertaining and school stander. New York is noted for these things as well as jobs. But the City that is suppose to be so good in many different fields is defaulting. I sit down and woulder how a city that is suppose to be good bussiness, commersial and entertaning wise could be let happen to us. This problem couldn't have just started. It had to started some years ago. And now the problem has I caught up with us. I say this too, that I believe the government and mayor of New York in the past had to see some of these problems coming before now. But problely tryed to cover up by shifting the budget around until they could do it any more. I also believe a lot of this has to do with taxes. Because everytime taxes are raised it causes the industers more

> money and soon or later they move there bussiness to another city. They can't aford to pay higher taxes. This causes a cut in money coming into New York. I think that if the government or state of New York don't get together and try to bring New York out of these crisis. It going to bring the standers of New York City and the nation down.

Louella's paper exhibits most of the characteristics of a basic writer. The errors of surface form—misspellings, poor agreement, ending problems, omitted words—are clear, although their causes may not be. So, too, with the logical tangles, the sentences like the first, which seems to start with one idea and move to another, and ends up losing both. Most of these problems had been discussed by Shaughnessy in terms of the nature and patterns of errors produced by basic writers, but Sondra Perl's work added a valuable dimension by showing us how such texts came into being.

By using the composing aloud technique, Perl was able to observe hidden aspects of her students' composing processes. This gave her a vivid picture of how they try to deal with the challenges of a college writing task. While she found many dysfunctional strategies, her most important discovery was that basic writers had functional and stable composing processes. Surprisingly, their composing processes were quite similar to those of their more skillful peers.

While they did do some percolating, the act of writing itself functioned as a process of discovery for them. They found out while writing what they wanted to say and would move backward and forward to further plan their emerging paper. They sometimes got into trouble through this strategy, as evidenced in Louella's opening sentence. It starts clearly:

> "I believe that the problem of New York City is"

but that problem is never fully spelled out. What seems to have happened is that Louella's personal outrage breaks through. When she mentions New York City it diverts her into the comment that it's "the hottest spot in the Nation" and so on. This kind of problem is solvable once we better understand its cause. Furthermore, writer's like Louella edit within and between drafts. They are very conscious of the importance of correctness, so worried about it, in fact, that on average by the time they've written *three words* of a sentence, they're sure an error must lurk there somewhere. This intrusive editing/correctness anxiety is entirely counter-productive. It helps account for some of the incoherency of the texts they produce, since their error worries overwhelm the flow of their ideas. And when they read over their texts for possible changes, they are most conscious of the need for surface corrections and rarely able to notice larger problems of clarity.

SONDRA PERL Although we've taught basic writers the rules for editing finished prose, those aren't the things that are going to help them throughout the process. These students read finished prose all the time and they think that it started out that way. There's a story about a teacher who showed a student a number of drafts of Richard Wright's when he was writing, I believe, *Native Son*. There were lots of changes and cross-outs and deletions. The student remarked, "Oh, look at all these cross-outs, he must be a lousy writer," as though correct writing is what happens right out of the pen. And I don't think teachers ever, or often enough, share with their students anything about their own composing process—that it's messy, that it's a jumble. And that professional writers, more often than not, go through many, many drafts before anything can be considered finished.

The basic writers' egocentric stance probably developed from getting little response to the content of their writing and much to its surface form. It also reflects their inexperience with genuine writing situations. One of the limits of Perl's work is that since she was trying to study how these students were performing in academic writing tasks—as opposed to a situation where the writer chooses either purpose or audience to a significant degree—we just don't know how they would do under other conditions. But it's clear that neither purpose nor, more strikingly, audience are consciously considered by basic writers.

Although we've drawn most of our examples of basic writers from those students who show up inadequately prepared for college writing, these people were basic writers long before they reached college. Basic writing problems appear very early and are clearly evident in upper elementary school and throughout secondary school. The earlier such problems are identified, the easier they are to solve.

If we're going to avoid creating more basic writers for the future, and if we're to design better instructional programs to get them on track, we must know as much as we can about what went wrong. What influences, positive and negative, causes these failures? Are they school related? home related? culturally related?

Although there has been some theorizing and research on these problems, much of it has been very indirect and inconclusive. One of the reasons for this is that with the exception of Loban's study (1976) of the same group of children moving from kindergarten through 12th grade, there are few longitudinal studies of writing development (and Loban's study doesn't focus on basic writers). We also have a large number of linguistic and sociolinguistic studies of related issues in the language development of people who are basic writers which have shed light particularly on the nature of nonstandard dialects and their effects on reading and writing. Our ideas are based on the best that is known about these problems, but much more inquiry is needed before the full picture will be revealed.

The most significant cause of breakdown which leads students to become basic writers appears to be poor instruction. The poor teaching is probably the result of the inadequacy of guiding pedagogical theories and the special difficulties posed by students who come to school speaking a different language from their mainstream peers. We learn to talk the variety of language that is spoken around us. The first linguistic source is the family, next the neighborhood, and eventually the broader community. Children come to school speaking that variety which is characteristic of their family and peers. And for every child, the language of home is, to some degree at least, different from the oral language of the school. Problems arise most frequently when the differences are greatest—as in the case of a Spanish-speaking child in an English-speaking school—but in some ways they're even more severe when the differences are substantial but not officially labeled—as with speakers of different varieties of English in a standard English-speaking school.

It's a commonplace among linguists that the distinction between a dialect and a language is a socio-political rather than a linguistic issue. Some differences among the linguistic systems of peoples are labeled as distinct languages (i.e., French, Spanish, or Italian), while similar distinctions aren't so labeled in such cases as the various varieties of Chinese. In English there are mutually incomprehensible varieties—ask any American who has been in Yorkshire—but no separate labels. The issue here isn't comprehension, but rather that "the English language" (or any language) is an abstract fiction. That is, no one speaks "the English language," but instead one of a number of dialects, that together make up "English." Even so-called "standard dialects" vary regionally—standard London English isn't standard Boston, Atlanta or Toronto English—and each variety has certain distinctive characteristics. In each region a child who comes to school speaking a nonstandard dialect for that region is likely to suffer some social and educational consequences.

Although some spoken dialects are closer to it than others, no one speaks Standard Written English (SWE). It's true that SWE varies less around the world than do its spoken counterparts, but everyone has to make some adjustments between their spoken variety of English and SWE. The task of learning to read and write can be defined as developing the appropriate rules which connect the way we talk to the representation of the language embodied in SWE. In speech, for example, most American English speakers delete a final consonant sound when the first sound of the next word is also a consonant. *Used to* is pronounced more like *use to* and many speakers write *would of* for *would have* or *would've.* In learning to read and write, we must learn to notice and/or produce such final consonants because they carry meaning which is, at least some of the time, non-redundant, and because whether or not the meaning is redundant, the conventions of SWE require it.

For a speaker of a dialect that deletes such final consonant sounds in all contexts even before a following vowel, e.g., *used a hammer* pronounced as *use a hammer*, learning the SWE representation may be harder. But it's not impossible if learner and teacher acknowledge the task and recognize that the connections can be learned without first changing the way the learner speaks. The appropriate connections between oral and written forms do exist, because both are systematic and rule-governed, but in order to be learned, the learning must be based on actual connections between the systems, rather than arbitrary determinations.

Not all basic writers speak a substantially divergent dialect from SWE, but many do. Schools don't help these students much when they insist on emphasizing surface correctness at the expense of fluency and clarity. This leads to a cycle of error-making/error-correcting/rule-learning which fails because the rules taught aren't the rules being broken. Instead, whatever effort needs to be placed on rules (or errors) should occur in the context of the actual errors and the actual systems that underlie those errors. Every student needs help in mastering the conventions of SWE, but that help will only be valuable if it connects the students' own language to SWE.

It's also important to recognize that every learner of SWE needs lots of productive experience with it as well as active reception. In fact, the most serious deficiency of all poor writers (and readers) is usually directly related to the paucity of time spent reading and writing as part of their educational lives. There are no easy ways to make writing and reading more significant for those writers who lack early and continuing involvement in these subjects, but that doesn't diminish the importance of trying to do so.

BARBARA GRAY The most simple and straightforward way of reducing dialect interference errors is to have students read a lot and write a lot to real audiences. The more exposure they have to written language, the more they'll develop what you call an "ear" for language. Even though it's not an ear for spoken language, they need to develop a special internal ear for how Standard Written English (SWE) sounds. Until they have that ear, it doesn't do them a bit of good (in fact, it misleads them) to say, "Just read this out loud and listen to the way it sounds and you'll see what's wrong with it."

The easiest and best way to deal with the problem of basic writers and basic writing is to avoid creating the problem in the first place. At least some of the problems can be eliminated by a more meaningful curriculum. But preaching the avoidance of bad teaching doesn't solve the problems of teachers who find themselves with a classful (or even a small group) of basic writers. What is a teacher to do?

The first step is diagnostic: find out as much as possible about what your students are doing and how they came to be that way. While the average working English teacher won't have either the time or the facilities to carry out a study such as Sondra Perl's, using the insights she's developed can help us figure out what's going on. Even if you can't have your students compose aloud, watching them write, timing various stages of the process, and collecting all of their notes, drafts, etc. can provide a revealing picture.

Some helpful diagnostic questions might be:

- How long does the writer engage in planning activity? What sorts of things does he do?
- Does the writer write each sentence fluently or are there lots of hesitations and changes made?
- How much editing goes on during drafts? What sorts of changes are made?
- Is there any evidence of global revising strategies (i.e., rearrangement of paragraphs, addition of whole sentences, deletion of clauses)?
- Is there any evidence of audience awareness? Of changes for improved clarity?
- If the writer reads his paper aloud, what sorts of differences are there between the written text and the pronounced text? What notice does the writer take of them?
- If more than one draft is written, what sorts of between-draft changes are made?
- What's the final text like? Errors in spelling? punctuation? coherence? logic? transitions? What sorts of strengths does it have?

The answer to such questions won't provide all the necessary information, but if observation is coupled with a writing conference/interview with the writer about his previous writing experience, attitudes toward writing, educational and career goals, and so on, the teacher should have an adequate picture of whom he's dealing with. Given the appalling numbers of students most of us meet daily, maybe such diagnostic procedures seem impossible, but in dealing with problems as severe as those of the basic writer, doing so is essential. And it is possible if the writing classroom is set up as a sort of writer's workshop.

It's not uncommon for basic writers to believe that all they really need is another good dose of the old reliable grammar medicine. Given their awareness of error and their concerns for correctness, they often believe that this time they'll really learn the rules and all will be well. Tempting as such a prescription might appear to them and to us, to accede to it is to deny our new understanding of the underlying problems of such writers. Anyone who still doesn't believe that should look again at Louella's paper on page 65 or at Tony's paper in Exercise 5 and actually or mentally correct all the surface errors. It seems clear to us that such papers, even if error-free, still don't work. Trying to help such writers control and express their ideas must precede worrying about getting the commas right.

Our attitude toward solving the problems of basic writers is that what they need is to unlearn much of what is harming their production processes—in particular trying to produce perfect texts the first time with the resulting interference in drafting by editing—and then to get them back on the developmental track with appropriate adjustments for their age, maturity, and life experiences. They aren't beginners, but they need to have successes in order to develop fluency before we can expect them to move on. It may be naive to believe that everyone can become a writer, but we're convinced that the developmental approach suggested in this chapter can make a substantial difference in the success rate of all schools with all students.

WRITING TO LEARN

1. The stories of Colleen, James, Jody, and Matt were all written in Katherine Becker's 2nd grade class. Read them and determine what they show about the fluency level each child has reached. Although your responses would be delivered orally to second graders, rather than in writing, briefly write the most important things that you would like to say to each writer.

THE DAY I ShOLD NOT HAVE RiDDEn MyBicycle

One day I got on my new bicycle for the

first time

I Started to go down the hill

very fast.

Suddenly a car came speeding up

the hill.

I tried to make a sharp turn
But since I was not so used to
it I crashed in to somebodys
yard.
I was okay

The End

Matt S.
I went to the hospidl wn I was young
I had the ammonia

Before I moved

Before I moved I lived in a little house.
It had a bathroom, three bedrooms, a kitchen
and a parler. But what I liked best was
my friends. I had so many friends.
Thir names were Mona, Ericka, Donna, Debby
and Christine. We had alot of fun
together. When the time came my
grandfather got old and we had to move.
I cryed when I had to say good-bye.
But I got to play with all of my friends
the day I moved. We played in the park
across the street we all had fun and drank
soda. THE END by Colleen

SKATING

By Jody Litwin

Skating is fun to do, you glide in the
air. Or you push and push and push and go
faster and faster and faster! And soon you
will fall and that's fun to. Then take
a brake and may be have lunch
and hot coco. Then go back on the
ice for a while and then go home
with mom and dad.

THE END

2. Lillian Buie was our student in the N.Y.U. Summer Abroad Program in 1978 in England and was enrolled in the Sunrise Semester course. An experienced high school English teacher, she was North Carolina teacher of the year in 1979. The following selection from her writings includes:
   a. Her introduction to us of some of her student Phyllis's journal entries;
   b. her comments to Phyllis on those journal entries;
   c. a letter published as part of Larry Cheek's column in the *Fayetteville Times,* but *not* written for publication;
   d. a poem.

   After reading them, write a brief response either to Lillian about her teaching or her writing or to us about the characteristics she shows which demonstrate her maturity as a writer.

Phyllis's Journal entries with teacher comments

Phyllis became a member of my poetry class at the beginning of our spring semester. She has a reading score of ninth grade, sixth month, which is about average for our school or perhaps somewhat above. She is 17 years old, a junior in high school. Her basic skills in writing are low, but she loves to write and keeps her journal enthusiastically. She is beginning to volunteer to read her entries to the class, who are enthralled by some of her stories. When she reads her writing aloud, it sounds good. When I attempt to read it later, I am constantly interrupted by illegibility and major errors in both spelling and punctuation. I'm encouraging her in sharing her thoughts, feelings, experiences by telling her to continue to write expressively. Then when she wants others to read her work instead of merely listening to her, we will work together to get it ready for an audience of readers. That will mean real concentration on spelling and on common-sense punctuation. I think, once motivated to overcome these handicaps, Phyllis is bright enough to teach herself through observation of printed materials. To encourage that independence I'm first working with her. One activity that seems to work is for me to read her journal to her in a dictation lesson. She listens to her own words, concentrating on ending sentences properly when I pause at the end of a complete thought or drop my voice after a statement, raise it for a question, show emotion for an exclamation. She also pays more careful attention to spelling, and her dictated draft is fairly correct in comparison to the original. It'll be interesting to see if she makes any real improvement during the semester or if she will remain "terabul at english."

Entry 1

. . . . today was our first day in poetry class and Mrs. Buie talked about her family and read some from her jurnel. When she talked about her son Jonjon I wanted to talk about Betty but I dont because Im afade the others in the class wont unnerstand and it hurts me when anybody acts like my sister isnt worth talking about or hardly a person at all and lookslike they dont wanna here about something like that, Im glad we have to write jurnels tho Im terabul at english and I wouldn't want anybody to see what I write but maybe I can talk like we did today. We have to tell about ourselves and know everybody's name and be friends befor we can get any grades and we are going to make scrapbooks and share those too.

teacher comment:

Phyllis, thanks for telling me about Betty. The class seemed to understand when I talked about Johnjon. They reacted just as I had hoped they would—quiet and thoughtful and thankful that they can read and write and *think*, as well as do the take-for-granted things like feeding and dressing themselves. I think they also seemed glad that Johnjon has someone to love him and isn't ashamed to talk about him, even if he can't do any of that. Hearing about your sister can help your classmates appreciate the things they can do; you can also help them feel love for those who are different. So *do* share Betty with the class. That way, you're doing something for you sister that she can't do for herself.

Don't worry about being "terabul at english." You're not—you think English, talk English, write English, even laugh and cry English. You might not be very good at spelling and punctuation; but when you really want people to share what you write and all the interesting English things that are in your head and heart, then you can clean up the mistakes. I bet after today, you'll start spelling TERRIBLE the way it ought to look! Looking carefully at stories and newspaper articles you read is one way to overcome writing problems.

entry 2:

Mrs. Buie said reading might help my writting and in a way it alredy has at least in making me want to write. I never liked reading alot until Roy Rogers and Dale evans came to Bett's school when we were living in Indiana and Roy gave Betty their picture and singed it and told about their retarded child Robin. He told about the book Dale had written and mama got it Angle Unaware and I read it and it made me cry but I loved it and I started reading alot of books and feeling like I wanted to share my feelings too. Ikept reading and reading and reading. Now I love to read and write and do alot of bothe. I'm gonna try to *look* at books harder so I can make my writing look the way it orta and make my feelings easy for other people to read but when Im writing fast to get these bubblingover feelings down I can't think about spelling and puntuation and all those English things.

teacher response:

Phyllis, the *most* important thing is to get all those "bubbling over feelings" down on paper so that you can look at them and deal with them. Gradually you'll be able to dwell on one thought at a time, and then you'll find the "traffic" signals of punctuation marks helpful both to you and to those who read your thoughts and stories. I'm glad you love to read and write; I do too. I think that's half the battle in becoming a successful English student. Those of us who really want to share experiences and ideas can pretty quickly pick up right ways to do it. Let's work together on your writing skills; you'll be proud of the results.

Johnjon—Special Child

Larry Cheek, *Fayetteville Times*, 1978

No one feels more keenly the pain of retardation than the mother who bears a retarded child.

Lil Buie of Wagram is such a mother.

"Thank you for your column on visiting the children at O'Berry," she writes. "As one who knows the heartbreak of having a retarded son as well as the joy of watching a healthy, bright son mature into an empathetic, concerned young man, I was deeply touched by your article.

"There isn't any story-book happy ending for the situation at O'Berry, one so typical of institutions anywhere, but awareness by the public is the first step toward amelioration of the problem.

"We haven't been able to make life abundant for Johnjon, who will live out his years in an institution, but he has made us aware of the tremendous need to do something in all areas—prevention, care, education and legisltation.

The Influence of Their Brother

"I don't yet know how much our four normal children will contribute to society, but I like to think that their motivations and goals will be influenced by their handicapped brother.

"I already know that Johnjon has been responsible for many of the programs for the retarded in Scotland County, and that is a great comfort to me.

"I'm enclosing a poem I wrote the year we made the decision to place Johnjon at Caswell—20 years ago.

"When we went down to visit him a year or so later, we took Jim and Hattie, a black woman who had nursed Johnjon in his infancy. She kept saying 'Jim, you may be your mama's boy but Johnjon is my boy.'

"Puzzled, four-year-old Jim finally whispered in my ear, 'Mama, what color is my brother?' Thanks again Larry."

Here is Lil Buie's poem, written after her retarded son had been placed in an institution, there to spend the rest of his life:

'So Quiet, So Still, So Small'

Come into the world, a weak, wailing child,
Often too meek, bashful, and mild;
From restless adolescence to womanhood arrived;
Became wife of one, mother of five.
Three lovely girls, one husky boy
To give life meaning, to bring us joy
But still searching for life's real code,
A guide for humanity, a post in the road.
And, Fate with its ironic turn
Brought me that lesson from a child who could never learn.
Our very special little boy, so quiet, so still, so small,
Receiving from life so little brought the most precious gifts of all.
For in loving him we learned to love all mankind.

The weak, the simple, the poor, the black, the blind.

'Twas he who taught us each man is our brother
Realizing through suffering we must love one another.

Life brought me much—this would I share
Words from a Book of wisdom rare:
Surely a little child shall lead thee;
In as much as ye do it unto the least of these,
Ye do it also unto me.

3. When Diane Hilser appeared on Sunrise Semester, she shared a poem with us and talked about how having a supportive and responsive group helped write it.

This Might Have Been(:)A Sonnet

After a long season of silence,
in a voice I had learned to distrust,
you came to carry away some things
and to chronicle on an afternoon's page
a short footnote to our history.
You left the shape of our clock in the hall,
ghosts of our prints against the wallpaper,
hollows on the shelves of our collected past
and clean patches on graying kitchen walls.
Knowing how fragile most things are,
you carefully wrapped what you had chosen
and packed these few things in some grocer's box.

I went upstairs and slept in our bed
while you dismantled our life together
and was pleased, when I awakened,
to find you crying in the kitchen.

Diane Hilser
1979

a. Write a brief, personal response to it which could be shared with other readers of the poem;
b. Consider it (and Lillian Buie's poem in # 2) as examples of teacher writing. Should such texts be shared with students? Write a brief position paper making a case for one side or the other.

4. In this chapter we take a strong stand on the uselessness of grammar teaching. Pretend that your school is deciding whether or not to buy a grammar/language series and that you've been asked to state your expert opinion. Write as powerful a statement as you can to the administration about your position. Needless to say, your view doesn't have to be ours. This will work best if you can focus on an actual book that can be specifically cited. (Is this a dummy run? Well, somewhat, but in our view, every English and language arts teacher has a professional responsibility to have a clear position on this issue.)
5. Consider the basic student paper by Tony. What are its major problems? How is it different from a beginning writer's paper?

Tony's Paper

All men can not be consider equal in America base on financial situations. Because their are men born in rich families that will never have to worry about any financial ~~diffuel~~ diffuliculties. And then they're are ~~the~~ / another type of amer/icans that are born to a poor family. And this is the type of Americans that ~~will~~ may / always have some kind of finanical diffuliculty. Espeical today ~~today~~ ~~the~~in new york The way the city has fallen ~~has~~ ~~fallen~~ into fin--debt. It has become such a big crisis for the ~~people~~ working people, in the If the working man is able to find a job, espeicaly ~~for~~ with / ~~city~~ the ~~a~~ city The way ~~the~~ ~~way~~ the city ~~is~~ / fin-sitionu is set up now, /He'll problely lose the job a whole lot faster than what he got it. When he loses his job he'll / have even more fin-difficulity. And then he'll be force to go/ to the city for some fini-assi-. So right here you can see that all men in America are not create equal in the fin-sense.

5

Writing to Learn Across the Curriculum

How We Can Learn Through Writing

One of the most important curricular developments of the last few years has been the emergence of concern for language, and, particularly, of writing, across the curriculum. Originally spotlighted in England by James Britton and his colleagues (see, for example, the Bullock Report, 1975; and Martin et al., 1976), it has recently become important in this country as well. Simply put it means: *The productive use of language, and especially writing, is a valuable tool for learning for all students in all subjects at all ages.* Writing to learn in social studies or science or industrial arts may not seem to be a vital interest of English teachers, but we hope to show in this chapter why writing across the curriculum *is* important and how English teachers can promote it in their schools.

The premise that writing can be a tool for learning depends on several concepts, one of which is this very broad understanding of writing: that it occurs any time one's mind is engaged in choosing words to be put on paper. It includes note-taking, list-making, writing down observations, and expressing feelings, as well as more traditional activities like writing lab reports, essay test answers, essays or stories. Central to this understanding is the notion of language choice. This excludes copying completely—which Bryant Fillion (1979) and Arthur Applebee (1981) have found occupies a lot of so-called writing time in schools. Writing that involves minimal language choices, such as filling-in-blanks exercises or answering questions with someone else's language—the textbook's or the teacher's—are of limited value in promoting either writing or learning.

Writing to learn depends upon an active rather than a passive approach to learning. It requires that we conceive of both learning and writing as meaning-making processes that involve the learner in actively building connections between what she's learning and what is already known. Research on the composing process has shown that writing is not a simple process of transcribing a predetermined text, but a complex process of discovery.

Writing's capacity to place the learner at the center of her own learning can and should make writing an important facilitator of learning anything that involves language. Writing that involves language choice requires each writer to find her own words to express whatever is being learned. Such a process may initially serve to reveal more gaps than mastery of a particular subject, but even that can be of immense diagnostic value for teacher and learner alike. And as the process is repeated, real and lasting mastery of the subject—and its technical vocabulary—is achieved.

This last point deserves emphasis. Achieving a rich and versatile vocabulary has always been one of the major byproducts of a genuine education. It's no accident that the verbal part of the SAT (which is, in many respects, a vocabulary test) has consistently been the best predictor of college academic achievement. Like most properties of the language system, a rich vocabulary is the result of productive language use, which includes active and responsive reading and listening as well as writing and talking, and is only partially susceptible to direct instruction. Most teachers know that direct vocabulary teaching has little or no permanent effect—it's the quintessential example of "learning" that vanishes immediately following the quiz—but they keep trying it anyway because they don't know a better method.

Writing to learn, to discover connections, to describe processes, to express emerging understandings, to raise questions and to find answers provides the best single means of making the acquisition of vocabulary an active and lasting process. The vocabulary itself isn't the explicit end of learning; rather, it's the means through which the learning is achieved and expressed. Without finding appropriate technical terms, one cannot explain in writing why Jackson vetoed the Second National Bank Bill, or describe how plants get food, or discuss how meaning is made in a Shakespearean sonnet, or write a recipe for fudge. Used in these ways, words become a natural part of the writer's permanent lexicon rather than being the property of the teacher or the text.

JOHN MAYHER What are the core theoretical ideas in a language across the curriculum program?

ROBERT PARKER The primary goal is not to improve students' talking and writing. The primary goal is to improve students' learning. Language in general and writing in particular are seen as the main instruments of learning. The focus on writing, whether in English or other subjects, is always on how writing might be used more widely, more effectively by students as a learning tool. Yet I'm convinced that if you set as your primary goal using writing as a means of learning, you will also improve students' writing.

Central to the idea of using writing to learn is the understanding that learning is promoted this way only if the writing is perceived as purposeful *by the writer.* If it's used largely for regurgitation, the writer is correct to see it as a purposeless dummy run which requires only minimal involvement and effort. But if the task is to describe what one has personally observed about, say, the behavior of a bird nesting in the student's backyard and if, further, the intended audience isn't only the teacher, then the writing and the learning take on a different character. The learning should promote a personal connection between what was observed and the theoretical lenses through which the observation takes place. The teacher (and the texts) help provide those lenses, but the student must do the observing, make the synthesis, and, most important, do it all by shaping a written report for his classmates.

The report must be personal, as well, since it, too, requires a synthesis between the technical language of science and the personal voice of a student speaking to other students. While it's true that students will eventually need to master science writing if they're going to become professional scientists, there's no need to do so in secondary schools. If they've really mastered the content through personal involvement, it's easy enough to help them later develop the ability to express it in impersonal terms. Requiring impersonal academese too early—we have found some teachers assigning research papers in fourth grade—encourages either copying or what we sometimes think of as verbal shortcircuiting, in which the words go in the eyes and out the pen without ever finding a permanent lodging in the brain.

JOHN MAYHER Why were you so unhappy with the fact that you found so much impersonal writing going on throughout the secondary school years in all subjects in Great Britain?

JAMES BRITTON Abstract and impersonal writing is the appropriate end product for writing in physics, biology, chemistry, social studies, history, and so on. That's the goal we're aiming at. But if you insist on that from the start—limp around in that kind of language until you can walk in it—then the learning process of moving from personal writing to more abstract never happens.

Another counterproductive way of attempting to use writing to learn is to place too much initial stress on correctness. This is particularly important for English teachers to convey to both colleagues and students, since writing can't be an effective tool for learning if writers must worry about spelling and punctuation from the first moment they put pen to paper.

Writing to Learn in Action

A natural kind of writing-to-learn assignment is to write about something we've just read. Although it's true that much of our education has been designed to remove any traces of personality from our writing, along with any confidence in our personal voice, for most of us that voice is there, somewhere, and will be revealed when we're no longer afraid of being censured for sounding like ourselves. The assignment we'd like you to try will require that kind of voice and will be free from any censure.

We ask that you write a brief response to the first section of this chapter. If you're reading this book alone, you'll be writing only to yourself, unless you can enlist a friend to read it; but the point is to clarify, extend, synthesize your understanding of our ideas, not necessarily to communicate them to anyone else. What do we mean by a response? Many forms seem possible:

- A summary of what *you* consider to be the important points.
- An example from your own experience of how some aspect of this works (or doesn't).
- An argument with us about some particular point (or points).
- A letter or note to a fellow teacher briefly giving the most significant points you think *they* would be concerned with.
- Some thoughts about how you might put some of these ideas into practice in your classroom.
- A description of how you're already using writing as a tool for learning in your classroom.
- A comparison of a "traditional" with a "writing-to-learn" method of teaching some concept.
- Some questions you have about something in the section.
- Or any other kind of response that seems useful to you as a means of strengthening, personalizing and extending the learning process that you began when you started to read this chapter.

This kind of response is quite different from the traditional "read the passage and answer the questions" pedagogy. There are some uses in asking readers questions after they've read something, but such questions in texts and on tests too often require more regurgitation than synthesis. As in reading tests, the clever student soon learns to read the questions first and then find the answer. While such behavior is clearly an efficient test-taking strategy, using it all the time makes schooling essentially one long test and has the consequence of limiting what is learned to what is tested. Sensitive teachers have blanched for years at the question, "Will it be on the test?" But we must all recognize that we've carefully taught our students to value test scores, and that in too many schools the continuous testing mode of teaching has reduced learning to expediency.

Part of the value of writing to learn, therefore, may be to bring back a broader and deeper commitment to learning for students and teachers alike. Doing so in the present climate of short-term accountability and back-to-basics may seem impossible, but we're convinced that students do want more out of schooling than they usually get and that contemporary critics of schools are not wrong in suspecting that improvement can be made, however misguided they may be in either diagnosis or prescription.

So write your response and reflect on the experience. Particularly, think about what and how you learned through the process of writing. When you've done so, look at some students using writing as a tool for their own learning.

Learning Logs

One of the most effective ways students can use writing as an aid to learning is to keep a running account of what's going on as they work in a particular course. Such accounts have often been called *content journals* (Fulwiler, 1980), but we prefer the term *learning logs*, which emphasizes the desired focus on keeping track of what and how one is learning. Like journals, these learning logs are written for oneself, but they're also an excellent forum for potential dialogues between students and teachers about where things are or aren't working. If teachers regularly skim each learning log, they can get a useful picture of what each student understands or doesn't understand about the material.

Getting started with learning logs requires explicit directions to students, a clear commitment of time and energy on the teacher's part, and enough discussion about what's happening during the first few weeks to ensure that students really do get with it. The best sets of directions we know of come from a school with a highly effective writing across the curriculum program coordinated by Cindy Rudrud in Tolleson High School, Arizona. Her general set of directions asks students to write in order to:

1. React to class activities—what did you think of a lab, a movie, test, etc. Was it valuable?
2. Describe yourself as a science, math, social studies, etc. student.
3. Explain new concepts and ideas. How does new information fit in with what you already know? (Audience is yourself in this case.)
4. Explain new concepts to another student. Identify various audiences—a younger student, a student who has been absent, for example.
5. Question the significance of what you've learned.
6. Question what you don't understand. Try to get material straight when you're confused.
7. Explain assignments in your own words.
8. Describe what has been said about the subject during class.
9. Explain why assignments aren't done on time.
10. Evaluate the teacher and the course content.

The list is varied and provides opportunity for introspection as in numbers 2 and 6, commentary on the course or class as in 1 and 10, and communication as in 4 and 7. Obviously some types will fit better with some activities or subjects than with others, but the common point about all of them is that they demand active, personal involvement of *each* student/writer in the processes and content of the course. Each helps forge a personal connection between the learner and the material that will enable the learner to become the master of the process. Too often students sit quietly in class with no idea of what's going on. A learning log, and the possible teacher-student dialogue, in private, can go a long way toward opening up otherwise mysterious subjects.

Another Tolleson teacher, Bonnie Thompson, who teaches chemistry and anthropology, has made effective use of learning logs. These are directions for her chemistry students:

"Think" Writing for Chemistry

- The writing you'll do in your chemistry log will provide a way for you to think about what you're learning, to question what you don't understand, and to integrate new concepts and ideas with what you already know. This writing will be *thinking* on paper; therefore, don't worry about mechanical correctness or spelling. Deal with ideas and questions instead. "Think" writing means:
  1. Summarizing what you've learned.
  2. Integrating new ideas with ones you already understand.
  3. Questioning the significance of what you learn.
  4. Discovering questions about what you know.
  5. Discovering questions about what you don't understand.
- "Think" writing will help you:
  1. Understand new material.
  2. Ask relevant questions.
  3. Make new knowledge part of you.
  4. Retain what you learn.
  5. Improve your ability to write in all subjects.
- When should you write? Write when:
  1. You're confused. Write to discover what specific points you don't understand.
  2. New concepts are introduced in class.
  3. You question the importance of an idea.
  4. You're preparing for a test.
  5. You're relaxed and in the mood to write.
- In the beginning you most likely will have to force yourself to write. Try to write at least three times a week.

Bonnie Thompson's emphasis on thinking on paper and her de-emphasis on correctness or spelling seem just right here. Although she was prepared for her students' initially having to force themselves to write, her patience and careful preparation of guidelines proved worthwhile. Before turning to some of the Tolleson think-writers, we should emphasize that the essential ingredient for a successful use of learning logs as a basis for student-teacher dialogue is trust between student and teacher. The dialogue between Ms. Thompson and a student named Brigette shows clearly that the necessary trust is operating, as does the frankness of the other entries which follow.

BRIGETTE: It's hard for me to understand how to do this but I'm getting there. I don't understand how to write the equation or how to write out the problem to solve the equation. That's mainly the problem. The test seemed pretty easy, but it looks like I got the answers wrong! Sometimes I feel like getting out of this class. I worry about my grades and it gives me so many headaches.
MS. THOMPSON: Don't—don't give up—even if you don't get a good grade you need the experience and satisfaction of hanging in there.
BRIGETTE: I guess a lot of it's my fault, I should come and ask you for help when I need it. I feel real stupid when I ask questions. Everyone seems so much smarter than me.
MS. THOMPSON: Don't you believe it!
BRIGETTE: It's dumb to feel that way. I know that! But I just do.
MS. THOMPSON: Fight it—your questions are the same ones they have too.
BRIGETTE: Science has always been this way for me. Hard! I don't know why, it just is. If someone explained it to me and told me why this has to be like this then I could understand it.

* * *

From Jim H's learning log

I understand most of the concepts that we've learned but that's not the problem. I often have trouble sifting things through my brain. I often have trouble writing an equation. I have trouble wondering which valence to use. For the most part I do understand most everything but writing the empirical formula. I keep forgetting how to figure out how many *moles* of this or how many moles of that there are. That's one thing I have trouble on.

* * *

From Vincente P's learning log

Mrs. Thompson:

I understand it all, so here's a little story.

Once upon a time, in a land far, far away, there was this compound. One day this compound met another compound and it was love at first sight. So after a short engagement, they bonded. They weren't a balanced equation. A few years later, they had baby elements and after years of bliss, they decomposed.

* * *

From Jim H's learning log

$Mg^{+2}Cl_2 + Ba^o \longrightarrow Ba^{+2}Cl_2 + Mg^o$

In this reaction the Magnesium is replaced by the Barium because it's more active. The Mg atom gains 2 e^- thus making it neutral. The 2 e^- gained by the Mg atom were lost by the Barium atom, thus making it a positive ion. Cl doesn't do anything in this section it just goes along for the "ride."

The best evidence of the value of keeping a learning log is in seeing them at work as in the examples above. But student perception is also important. Two of Ms. Thompson's students expressed their reactions powerfully:

From Ray O's learning log

Since this has been in effect, I've learned more in a short amount of time than since the start of the year. Everything is starting to come *clearer*.

See, what I used to do is a photo-copy type thing—just remembering what was going to be on the test but I didn't know *why*. I had learned it. Even though I sometimes got good grades or bad I still didn't know what was the purpose of learning—for example, the electrons on the outer shell or inner. I still have a problem doing that, but that was before the journals came in. Since journals have been in effect I'm starting to understand *why* AND that was the main problem. This idea of journals is a brilliant and fascinating idea. I thank those who thought up this idea and you for taking time to listen to us.

* * *

From Bob G's learning log

This journal has got to be the best thing that's hit this chemistry class. For once the teacher has direct communication with every member of the class. No matter how shy the student is they can get their lack of understanding across to the teacher. Some students are really embarrassed to raise their hand to ask a question in class. These journals act as a "hot line" to and from the teacher. I feel this journal has helped me and everyone that I know of in this class. The only thing wrong is, we should have started these on the very first day of school!! In every class!! Thank you very much for all the help this journal has been to me.

Not every teacher or every student will have such a positive experience with learning logs. But "think" writing can work as a tool for learning, and if more teachers will attempt it, more students will have an opportunity to understand *why* and to explore and strengthen their own processes of "sifting things through [their] brain."

The Place of Writing in the School Environment

What we must help teachers in other content areas see is that we're not asking them to become teachers of writing. They will, in fact, be helping their students learn to write because the only way we learn to write is by writing, but they must be encouraged to see writing as a *means* of achieving *their* objectives, not as an end in itself. The important thing for them and their students must be what is to be learned in a particular discipline. They shouldn't think of writing as yet another curricular burden imposed on them because English teachers are trying to shirk it.

We're not denying our mandate for writing instruction. Rather, we're recognizing the diversity of the kinds of writing which will be demanded of students in the real world and in academia. Few English teachers have the technical knowledge to guide students in learning to write science lab reports, electronics technical manuals, analyses of the causes of the Civil War, or guidelines for proper nutrition. Since writing well in a variety of modes is one of the most complex of human achievements, students need practice and help in all areas of the curriculum to be able to develop their writing competencies. Furthermore, some types of writing and learning are uniquely the province of English teachers. Teachers who are interested in having their students master their subjects in a way that makes them a permanent part of their storehouse of knowledge and skill will find writing-to-learn a valuable resource.

JAMES BRITTON It's more difficult to convince teachers that writing is a learning process than it is to convince them that talk is, because so often teachers use writing as a way of testing. They use it to find out what students already know, rather than as a way of encouraging them to find out. The process of making the material their own–the process of writing–is demonstrably a process of learning.

When we're looking for the appropriate place to use writing in the school environment we must first look at those areas of the curriculum that include a language component. In physical education, for example, this would be that part of the course where rules of a game are explained or a player's responsibilities detailed. In mathematics, the language component might be defined as the non-numerical part of learning math; that is, in solving and writing word problems, in writing out the steps one goes through to solve an equation, and, finally, in those areas where applications of math concepts to real world situations are taught. In industrial arts one might point out that writing instructions for machine operation, compiling a list of building materials, or displaying one's work with a description of how and why it was built all comprise the language component for such a course.

Finding the language component in each discipline is the key to convincing our colleagues that writing might be one way in which their students will be better able to learn these subjects. We don't want to rob students (and teachers) of the time for content, as such. In our experience, it's been fruitless to try to convince physical education teachers that writing in volley ball is worthwhile, unless we can show them that we're not replacing the actual physical activity with something as academic as writing. That's where the "language component" notion becomes so essential. When we've gotten teachers to concentrate on the language of their disciplines, we've been much more successful in getting them to accept using writing as a way for their students to learn.

Content area teachers argue that they're responsible for covering a certain amount of material and that adding writing to their curriculum will make coverage even less likely. Some of this coverage mania is tied to externally developed achievement tests, and until we can do something about these, crammed curriculums will continue to be a problem for all of us. But it's also tied up with standards for promotion from one grade to the next. These reside in a sequential model of learning which assumes that students have mastered, for example, the principles of simple computation in Grade X which will be the basis for learning algebraic concepts in Grade Y. This would be fine if it really happened. The problem is that it often doesn't.

When confronted with teachers who use the coverage issue to defend their stand against using writing, we've asked them if they believe their students are, if fact, learning the content of their courses. Usually the answer is "No," or "Not all of them are." These honest teachers admit that even though they're covering the required material, they know that some students are still lost in Chapter 2, although the rest of the class has moved on to Chapter 8. Asking this question is the best way we have found to break down the "coverage barrier." If students aren't learning, why race through all the required material? There's no good answer, which helps bring the discussion back to learning and away from "covering."

Once the discussion returns to learning, writing can be viewed more appropriately as one tool for that learning. Some of the best ways we know of using writing in the content areas are directly related to learning content. Take a math example. Writing summaries of chapters, writing up questions in response to new material, rewriting the steps in solving a problem to reveal where one's thinking goes awry, writing one-sentence summaries of a classroom discussion—all are ways of including writing in math.

Through summarization, explication, or formulation of questions, this writing is geared to discovering what students have learned, how much they've understood of what we've taught them and, most importantly, what we need to teach again. A lot of time is wasted in school in reteaching concepts that were supposed to have been learned somewhere else (often in a lower grade) or, in fact, have been learned. Writing can be a way of revealing both of these factors: we can help students learn better and retain knowledge better if they write about it; and a real benefit for us as teachers is that through students writing about something we can find out what they know and don't know.

Another reason content area teachers cite for not wanting to include writing in their classrooms is that they're not qualified to teach it. What they usually mean is that they've not been trained to edit students' work or don't have the expertise to correct spelling, punctuation, or other surface features. And they're right about this. That's why it's so important to make sure they understand that no one expects them to be writing teachers, but rather to provide a better way for their students to learn what they're teaching. We aren't asking them to edit their students' work, but to view writing as a genuine communicative activity, which means we do want them to demand clarity in students' writing.

Take history teachers as an example. History teachers, in general, believe they do require a fair amount of writing in their classes; they give essay tests and assign term papers. A widespread gripe, however, is that their students don't often write clear, full essay answers. The common response to this, we're told, is to accept these "short-circuited" answers because they are decipherable; the implicit connections can be figured out. Furthermore, content area teachers seem to believe that it's the English teacher's job to teach students how to write essay answers. We don't believe this. It isn't reasonable to expect that English teachers have the expertise in science, history or economics necessary to teach students what a well-written essay answer would be in these subjects. The more appropriate place for teaching students how to write essay test answers would be in the content areas themselves. Teachers across the curriculum would be wise to share both good and bad answers with their students, to discuss ways of writing these answers, and how to organize the limited time of an essay test to their best advantage so that the answers produced are clear and complete.

We suggest that teachers no longer accept incomplete or unclear answers;

that they demand clear and complete writing from their students. If students aren't given time to edit—and essay tests usually have tight time limits—they can't be expected to do it. On the other hand, we can insist on clarity. For teachers to use writing as a learning tool they must be able to ascertain from the writing what learning has or hasn't gone on. If the writing isn't clear, learning probably didn't happen. If learning did occur, yet the writing isn't clear, teachers still can't be sure. The two are so tied together that it seems ludicrous to demand one without the other. The final point is that content area teachers have all the expertise necessary to determine clear from unclear writing in their disciplines. They're qualified to require clarity and to teach it.

The third major reason our colleagues don't want to have students write more is usually unstated but nonetheless real: a genuine fear that they may be overwhelmed by an unending flow of student papers. It's true that reading student papers takes more time than scoring a multiple choice test, but many types of student writing (like the learning logs and others mentioned earlier) don't require extensive teacher feedback. And most of the techniques recommended for helping English teachers deal with the paper load can be adapted for use in other areas as well.

JAMES BRITTON What we mean by language across the curriculum is getting teachers who are teaching history and biology and social studies and so on to think more about the role of language in their lessons. In history, we learn to get historical perspectives on the world we live in; in geography and science, we get an organization of our experiences of the environment in different sorts of ways. These are all concerned with organizing the objective aspects of our experience. We have to show them that this isn't basically a concern for language. It's a concern for the quality of learning in all subjects. The quality of learning in all subjects might well benefit if teachers took more into account the actual talking and writing processes as learning processes.

If there's a message for teachers in general from this idea of language across the curriculum it's this: learning involves ability to put an idea into your own words. Rote learning, of course, doesn't. Rote learning means you can get high marks or give back what the teacher has given you whether you understand it or not. Credit is given for verbal expressions that don't necessarily involve understanding. Teachers are using writing to test whether a student has learned something rather than using it as a means of hastening that learning.

Writing Assignments Across the Curriculum

One of the most effective ways of helping teachers in other disciplines become convinced of the potentials of writing to learn is to get them to participate in the three-step process sketched below. The goal is to get other teachers to consider the value of writing as a means of learning content and skills that *they* define. Before or during the process there should be some discussion of the kinds of issues we've been addressing here.

As a first step, ask your colleagues to:

> ***Define a learning objective in your discipline which is appropriate for your students.***

It's true that not all learning is facilitated by writing, and so you might be wise to concede this in advance and ask them not to try to deliberately choose one that won't work. The goal is to think of broader and more original types of uses of writing to learn. The objective itself must be genuine.

After discussing the objectives (and trying to be sure they are objectives rather than activities, a confusion we've frequently encountered when we've done this), the next step is to ask the teachers to:

> ***Frame a writing task or assignment which would help students achieve the specified objective.***

The focus at this stage should be on *learning,* not writing. Effective assignments will require that both the student purpose and the intended audience are explicitly defined.

Before teachers do the first two steps, provide them with an example or two so that everyone is clear about what is intended and required. One we've used with some success is giving directions or instructions for how to get somewhere or do something. Such assignments can reveal how students understand a process in a specific subject area, which can range from how to make lasagna to how to solve quadratic equations. One form that the writing can take is a how-to instruction to be written for someone who doesn't yet know how. This assignment can take a variety of forms from writing the rules of a game, recipes, instructions for how to operate a machine, writing directions for doing laboratory experiments, or even how to write a term paper. Such assignments, labeled "consequential tasks" by Scardamalia, Bereiter and Fillion (1981), have a built-in sense of audience—someone who doesn't know how to do whatever it is—and purpose—the audience's need to know how. And they have a built-in check on whether or not they've been successful: someone can try to follow the directions and the writer can find out immediately whether they've been clear and complete by observing the efforts of the person who's following them.

They also have a built-in organizational structure, that of a step-by-step chronology. This is a great advantage for the inexperienced writer. There are ordering decisions to be made; the directions must specify that the frammis holder is assembled before the frammis is put into it and so on, but the major decisions involved in this type of writing and thinking are those that concentrate on being sufficiently sensitive to what the reader does and does not need to know.

These examples of consequential writing assignments lead to the third stage in this process, asking teachers to define:

> ***What criteria would you use to determine whether or not the learning had been accomplished?***

Several ideas intersect here. Most important is that stress is on the learning, not the writing. A good related question to ask is: How do the learning criteria relate to criteria for evaluating the writing? The conclusion should be that the criteria for evaluating the writing are *means* criteria while the learning evaluation deals with the desired *end.*

To illustrate this we've chosen another example which demonstrates a very different type of writing, but one which can still be used in writing-to-learn. The type of writing we have in mind is a story or narrative. The objective is from social studies: *to help students understand the interactive roles of geography and culture.* This is pretty highfalutin educationese, but we wanted it abstract so that it would be more adaptable to different age levels. A good objective would need to be more sensitive to the particular students involved. (This activity was designed for use in Arizona, but it could be adapted in various ways for other areas of the country.) The kind of writing we had in mind was a *what-if* story, or more specifically, the following:

> Imagine that you were one of the early British settlers in North America. You'd sailed from England in the late 17th century and had been part of a group determined to found a new colony farther inland than the first ones which had been established along the coast.
>
> For the purposes of this assignment, however, you're to imagine what is now the United States as though it had been reversed so that the West Coast is nearest to Europe. The colony our group hopes to found, therefore, is to be located in what is now Arizona.
>
> Your task is to write an eyewitness account of some aspect of the process of setting up such a settlement. You can concentrate on any part of the situation you would like to (i.e., travel difficulties, climate, encounters with the Native Americans, agriculture, the economy, or whatever), but remember you're trying to write a story which will be both interesting to your classmates and as true as possible to the situation such a group would have found if the geography of North America was so rearranged.

This assignment may not be everybody's idea of fun, but it does have many of the characteristics essential to a writing-to-learn assignment:

1. It requires imaginative thinking.
2. It stimulates and provides a reason for the acquisition of new knowledge.
3. It builds on the knowledge and experiences the students already have (in this case, of the climate, flora and fauna, and geography of Arizona).
4. It provides an accessible and enjoyable way of synthesizing old and new knowledge.
5. It provides a natural audience for the written work, which includes but isn't limited to the teacher.
6. It has clearly defined evaluation criteria for both the learning—in this case, the relation between the facts as presented in the story with what is known about *both* the characteristics of the 17th century British settlers and the conditions they would have found in 17th century Arizona—and the writing: is the story enjoyable to read, clear in its organization, and expressive of its point or message?

This last point about criteria relates directly to the evaluation/paper-grading problem. Teachers in other fields, as we've said earlier, will be reluctant to create a mountain of papers to read and grade. This isn't the place to suggest how to reduce that burden, but we hope it's clear that many writing-to-learn assignments don't require significant teacher time to evaluate. The consequential nature of writing directions, for example, can mean that the evaluation amounts to the student's observing how well they can be followed. The varied types of preliminary writing required for successful completion of the British settler story, including notes and early drafts, and the fact that the primary and most significant responses to the story should be from the class, will ensure that the teacher's task is manageable.

The primary value of writing-to-learn should be for the student. Through writing-to-learn, students can develop the capacity to evaluate whether or not they've learned the material. By placing them at the center of their own learning, we are potentially reducing their dependence upon us for validation of their worth as students. Much valuable writing-to-learn takes place in notes and logs and journal entries whose sole audience is the writer and whose sole purpose is to help her discover meaning and privately evaluate her progress.

If we're to be in the business of education rather than that of schooling, one of our long-range goals must be to help students become life-long learners. Developing their ability to use writing-to-learn and their confidence and enjoyment in the process and its results should then be one of the highest educational priorities. Learning is the quintessential human activity. Language is the most powerful learning tool we have. All students have a right to discover—or, perhaps, rediscover—the joys of learning, and we should all recognize that writing-to-learn is one of the best means of helping them to do so.

ROBERT PARKER There are a series of questions I think teachers across subjects could ask themselves about the kinds of assignments they give to their students.

1. Are there opportunities for students to be involved in the formulation of writing assignments?

2. Does the specific writing assignment encourage students to connect what they already know with the new material, the new information, the ideas which they're being presented with in a particular subject?

3. Does the assignment encourage students to reconstruct the new knowledge, the knowledge they're supposed to be learning? Does it encourage them to use this knowledge in some way?

4. Does the writing assignment represent, or is it located in, a genuine communication situation? Are students writing, at least at times, to truly communicate something to someone else, rather than being asked to write something consistently for an audience that knows the answers better than they do?

What we have said thus far can be applied throughout the curriculum and across grade levels. In the following sub-sections we look more closely at specific writing assignments in math and science, the arts, and social studies. The purpose of including these assignments is to provide a focus for discussion of better writing assignments with teachers in all areas of the curriculum. Each of them should provoke thought and increase awareness of the possible use of writing as a tool for learning in all subjects.

In discussing these assignments and the whole idea of writing across the curriculum with your colleagues, you might raise the following questions as a point of departure for developing additional assignments.

1. Who is the audience?
2. What's the purpose of this writing from the students' point of view?
3. To what degree is the student making language choices?
4. How do you plan to evaluate the learning?
5. Sequencing: What was necessary to prepare students for the writing and where do they go from here?

Writing Assignments in Math and Science

Math. The objective of this math assignment is to understand the Pythagorean theorem in geometry. It's loosely based on the television series,

"You Are There."

> Walter Cronkite has been given the assignment to report to the world the startling discovery of the Greek mathematician Pythagoras that the square of the hypotenuse of a right triangle equals the sum of the square of the other two sides.
>
> Write a transcript of the interview between Cronkite and Pythagoras which explains this discovery to a world which has never heard it before.

Such an assignment, coming after the theorem had been introduced to the class, would disclose whether or not students understood the theorem, had not just memorized the formula. In order for them to prove they understand it, they would have to be able to write an interview which detailed not only the appropriate steps for computing the theorem, but the reasons for the steps as well. The general audience are those people who have never heard of the theorem, but a better audience might be fellow students in the class who would have to solve a problem based on the process described in the interview. Thus, an evaluation check is built into the assignment. Because this theorem is a building block upon which more sophisticated math concepts will be erected, if the students don't show an understanding of it, they'll probably have a difficult time moving on.

Math at any level provides the best built-in evaluations we know of. When we ask students to write their own word problems, for example, we suggest that they work in groups of three. One person writes the problem; another solves it; and the third evaluates what happened: Could the second student solve it? If not, why? Was it because the problem was written poorly—concepts left out or inappropriate sequences of facts given—or was it because the second student doesn't understand how to solve the problem? This evaluation could be written up. The students then change roles so that each of them gets a chance to experience all facets of the writing. Later they will be prepared to challenge other groups with a problem they've created.

Science. The objective of this assignment, "Mr. Wizard Revisited," is to get students to distinguish among the various states of matter. It presupposes that younger students are available so that the older ones may use them as audience.

> Suppose you've been selected to be a guest speaker at "Metropolis Elementary School." You'll be required to introduce the subject of states of matter to a group of fifth graders by giving them directions for performing an experiment. Keeping your audience in mind, write a draft of the talk. Once your talk has been completed the fifth graders will attempt the experiment. (For example, having them melt a piece of ice, heat the liquid that results and observe what happens.)

The study of science demands a great deal of observation. To understand what one observes and to apply the theory to an experiment, students must be able to express in their own words what they thought was going on. Having students produce an experiment based on this presumed knowledge and understanding provides another built-in evaluation: Can the experiment be produced accurately based on the talk—on the students' knowledge of theory and understanding of the various states of matter?

Writing and Learning in the Arts

Language Arts We're including as part of the arts the language arts curriculum. The first assignment is to be used in a reading/literature class. The object of this assignment is to have students understand the role of prediction in the reading process.

> Here's the first paragraph of a short story. After you've read it, think about what might happen next, and write the rest of the story. (Be prepared to share your completed stories with your classmates.)

The teacher would then have students share their stories with each other before reading them the rest of the original version. The discussion might raise the following questions: How did student "predictions" match the outcome of the original story? What role does the language of the text play in being able to predict accurately? Why were some of the students able to predict better than others? Which story (a student's or the author's) does the class prefer and why?

Although the object is to help students learn how to predict and to understand the importance of prediction in the reading process, this is never made explicit. As far as they're concerned, their assignment was to come up with a story—one that would be as good as (maybe even better than) the author's—which they were to share with their classmates. The assignment challenges the students to a sort of duel with the author, where the student gets the chance to participate in the author's writing game. We don't think there's any way to fail here: whether the students match the author's story or create their own, they're still operating as if they (the author and student) are equals. We've often heard students say they could write a better story than this or that author they've read, and this assignment gives them the chance.

Art The following writing assignment was done with two high school freshman art classes in Tucson. The class had been drawing portraits, and the teacher was having some problems getting her students to understand how personality, or inner qualities, could be expressed through portraiture. When she asked us to teach her class, we attempted to solve the problem by showing the relationship between a "written portrait" and a "drawn portrait." Our objective was to show how words, like particular shadings or lines or emphases on a particular physical characteristic, can expose some inner quality of personality.

Teachers should first read several examples of "written portraits." We chose the Santa Claus description from "The Night Before Christmas" as one of our selections. This was easily recognizable—the students knew immediately who was being described, which gave them confidence to try others. Discussion of who this person might be and why would be helpful. Also, trying to get students to talk about the qualities that were implicit in the description would be necessary so they could become accustomed to how the writer achieves this. Then they, as artists, might be able to reproduce it in their own work.

Students were asked to write out their own descriptions of someone they knew well, or someone they liked, or someone famous—real or fictional. They were paired up and exchanged their written descriptions. Each was to draw the person from their partner's description.

Although there was mixed success in the final drawings—some were very good, others not—the students were challenged and learned a great deal. When their partners were unable to reproduce their written personalities accurately, the students realized it was in part their own lack of skill in expressing in words what they knew to be the person's true qualities. They understood that portrait drawing involves more than a simple line-for-line reproduction of facial characteristics. Even though writing wasn't the goal, the students were deeply involved in the writing part of this assignment and, even more important, actually saw the value in precise word choice and the power words can have in a subject like art.

Writing in Social Studies

We've used this assignment in in-service workshops for two reasons: 1) to get teachers to do some writing of their own; and 2) since this assignment is best done in groups, to familiarize teachers with group writing dynamics. One of the advantages of this assignment has to do with its writing roles: students adopt a character from the cast list and write from that character's point of view. For some reason, writing from a personality other than our own seems to have a loosening effect on writers. Because you're someone else, you don't feel as threatened as you would if you were writing in your own voice. Students have an easier time getting into the language of the period and the tone of the character they've chosen. Some roles required students to write a persuasive or argumentative piece, yet they were never told to write in a particular rhetorical form. It came naturally out of their chosen role. Again, this natural inclination caused less fear in students than if they were told to write a persuasive essay. Our ultimate goal for improving student writing is to get them to be comfortable with their own voices and confident that they have something worthwhile to say, but this assignment can be used early on and might be thought of as a way of enhancing fluency.

The time: June, 1776. The place: Philadelphia. The Second Continental Congress has met to discuss and decide on the Question of Independence, or as John Adams called it, "independency."

The Cast: This could vary depending on the focus the teacher wishes to give it. But you will need as many varying points of view as possible, i.e., a pro-slavery, an anti-slavery, a pro-independence, or an anti-independence. *Delegates:* Brief biographical sketches and points of view for each cast member should be included here.

John Adams
John Dickinson
Ben Franklin
Charles Carroll

Observer/Reporters: Same biographical sketches here.

Thomas Paine
Marquis de Lafayette
General Benedict Arnold
Abigail Adams

A draft of a Declaration written by Thomas Jefferson of Virginia has been circulated among the delegates for their consideration. (The teacher would hand out whatever Declaration paragraphs were pertinent. We used the two opening paragraphs of the Declaration; the paragraph dealing with the slave issue, which was eventually excluded; and the concluding paragraph.)

Your task is to assume the persona of one of the cast (each group, if there are enough students to make more than one, should divide this up), and write a brief position paper/report/argument on your own behalf. You may choose one of the following audiences to address: (Depending on the cast you've chosen, these audiences might change. The point here is to provide enough diversity of audience and to vary the types of forms possible so that students get a chance to experiment, and not everyone uses the letter-writing category.)

	Fellow Delegate	*Family Member*	*General Public*	*Government Official*
J. Adams	X	X		
J. Dickinson	X		X	
B. Franklin	X		X	
C. Carroll	X	X		
T. Paine			X	
Lafayette			French Public	French Court
B. Arnold				British Army
A. Adams			X	George Washington

> Write a statement expressing the position you've taken in a way that's appropriate to your chosen audience and consistent with your character and his/her private voice.

This assignment works best at the end of a unit or semester. Students will need background information about the topic which will require them doing additional research. Often we don't give students enough information or directions for an assignment. One of the things we've learned from using writing across the curriculum is that teachers must be clearer about what they want done and how, if they're to help students improve. One additional remark about this assignment as it pertains to social studies: students have a hard enough time connecting to a year ago; it's far more difficult to reach back with them to 1776 when we're trying to get them to understand their history. By involving them in this kind of writing assignment, where they *become* the people they're studying, students seem to have an easier time—and a more successful experience with history—than they would if we were to ask them in an essay exam to list the causes of the Civil War.

This kind of assignment also lends itself quite well to oral role playing, a valuable language development activity in its own right. When students get involved with using someone else's voice and persona, they can stretch their linguistic resources without fear of ridicule. Furthermore, and perhaps even more important, either oral or written role-playing activities provide for incidental learning about, say, the qualities of John Adams' personality or his relations with his peers, which provides a human context for understanding the events in which he participated. The not-so-secret secret, once again, is to enable the learner to make a personal connection between what she knows and what she is finding out. Building such language bridges through drama, talk or writing can transform the dry curriculum into personal living knowledge.

Search and Research: What Is the Role of the "Research" Paper in Schools?

One of the most discouraging aspects of talking with teachers about student writing is to be reminded of how much time is being spent on "research" papers or "reports." While this phenomenon is most apparent in high schools, it characterizes considerable writing instruction as early as grades three or four. In many cases it's virtually the only kind of writing done in the "content" areas of junior and senior high schools.

Such assignments are at best useless and more often counterproductive. They encourage copying rather than original thinking. They're rarely based on real questions that students ask. They're unconnected to anything the student knows or is learning. They ususally require excessive attention to form (footnotes, bibliographies, etc.) with much less focus on ideas. And they're too often exclusively focused on library-based information-gathering rather than on encounters with the real world through observation, experimentation, or interviews.

Much of this goes on, particularly in high schools, because of a misguided belief that colleges require it. Although some colleges do place considerable emphasis on matters of form and style for documentation, the use of such forms is usually seen as means, not ends; to deal with them otherwise distorts their function. The best outline, the most complete set of 3 x 5 cards, and the most scrupulous adherence to manuscript conventions will not substitute for asking real questions and developing clear answers.

Students must learn to give evidence for their assertions. This in turn requires that they know what sorts of evidence count. The growing ability to use and support generalizations is one of the learning objectives of secondary schooling. The shift from sterile research papers to evidence papers based on real inquiry would be a dramatic one, particularly if methods other than library research are permitted, even encouraged. This is probably the most vital shift of all: toward observation, interviews, surveys and the like as sources of data and support for generalizations. Students will eventually turn to books and magazines for information, but getting them there by means of a personal connection will encourage their learning the spirit of inquiry along with whatever the particular topic may be.

Real questions and real data gathering and analysis methods are much less likely to encourage direct copying or other forms of plagiarism. If we can't emphasize the *search* rather than the *re* of research, it would probably be better to abandon the research paper altogether.

A Better Approach

Many teachers may object that they do try, but students just aren't interested. Without delving further into the sources of student apathy (but aren't we in part to blame?), it seems clear that students will be more interested in questions that relate their own interests and experience to what they're investigating than in a pre-assigned set of topics coupled to a rigidly formal format. Examples of the kinds of questions we've heard students ask include:

- Why are so many old people moving to Arizona?
- Why do I have to stay in school 'til I'm 16?
- Since I can buy a pocket calculator for under $10.00, why do I have to learn the multiplication table?
- How do video games work?
- What kind of writing skills do employers really demand of high school graduates?

While we're all for library research (and some of these questions demand it), it must be seen as only one source of potential data. The kind of oral tradition, history, and interviews collected by Eliot Wigginton's students in the *Foxfire* books and other direct means of data-gathering will be both more involving and more likely to lead to permanent learning than exclusive reliance on traditional approaches. In the last question, for example, a survey of actual employers can be taken to determine their views on the importance of writing.

Learning is, after all, what research is supposed to be all about. The key ingredient of the research paper is that the writer learn from the experience. And, like all writing, it's more important that the writer communicate her learning than produce an empty, error-free paper.

Writing Research Papers

The following assignment, whose objective is to help students learn how to ask appropriate and meaningful questions for doing research and discover ways of carrying through on it, is one we've used several times in in-service courses for elementary and secondary teachers. The success we and the teachers have had with it has convinced us that beginning with personal inquiry is the best way of moving toward more formal academic searches, whether the children are in 3rd grade or 12th.

Students should be grouped in two's or three's to brainstorm a list of questions they would like answered by their classmates. After a number of questions are formulated, the group should review them for common properties, eventually narrowing the list to, say, five. If, for example, all the questions but one are about age, sex, number of siblings, etc., then the one on the number of books read during the year would be dropped, since it doesn't fit into the focus of the research—an ethnographic study of the class perhaps.

The implication for the first stage of the assignment should be clear: learning how to narrow a topic—always a difficult part of any writing assignment—can be learned practically and purposefully; learning what kinds of questions relate to each other, building toward a general thesis statement, provides good experience in organization skills; students can find other audiences besides their classmates to use in their research—other classes and community or family members; and their questions can also be used as a basis for searching out material in books and magazines or pamphlets.

Once questions are decided on and written up, each group interviews all other members of the class to collect their data. When the data is collected, the groups reconvene to collate it. From this material, the groups will then construct some kind of visual representation—say a chart, or a graph, or a map—of their findings. Finally, the groups will write up summary statements of their findings, including a general statement of what they were looking for and what they found; any inconsistencies in their findings; any trends they discovered from their answers, etc.

The main goal of this assignment is to get children excited about discovering things. Having seen this assignment in action ourselves, we can tell you that the teachers we worked with also got excited when the results start coming in. The students (and the teachers) couldn't always predict beforehand what they were going to find out and often were genuinely surprised. Sometimes they discovered that they hadn't asked enough questions, or that some questions were inappropriate to their overall "research design," or that the answers stimulated more questions they would have liked answered. All of these things made them even more eager to pursue further research.

Another major goal was making the connections between the collected data, the visual representation, and the written statement on it. Although students are given some instruction in school on the use of graphs and charts (there is even a section on the Math part of the SAT on graphs and charts), the material is never their own, so they never get to see how you transfer the information from one mode to another. This assignment creates a real context for such learning, and the more students do it, the better able they become in choosing the appropriate kinds of graphs for representing their work and for writing the best summary of what they've found.

One final goal for this assignment is to help students learn how to ask questions, to find out what questions are appropriate for the kind of research they want to do; and overall to learn how to construct a valid and interesting research project. What better way for them to do it than to learn by doing it themselves—to discover, as the teachers we worked with did, that you can't find out what fits or doesn't fit until you actually try it on for size?

A Final Challenge

A deadening aspect of too many American secondary schools is that there's virtually no academic interchange across departmental lines. In some schools there isn't even any within departments. Too many teachers go to work, close the door, and do whatever they do with no professional adult contact at all. One of the great potential impacts of a writing across the curriculum approach is that it provides a forum for the kind of professional talk essential to a dynamic school environment. Even disagreement and dispute can be healthier than silence and isolation.

A school's administration must be involved and supportive for a formal program to work. But tactically and practically, the best way to start such a program is with the small group of people who you know are interested and willing to try. Osmosis and subversion are probably more effective initially than confrontation and revolution. If the program begins to catch on, even an unsympathetic administration will come around. Even with a supportive administration, the idea of working slowly and with small groups probably still makes better sense than the kind of big in-service production that leads to little change but great resentment.

While we're preparing to tackle our colleagues in other departments, we should also make sure that our own house is in order. Each English department should look at itself to see how much writing-to-learn is going on. English departments do ask students to write, but how much of that writing is intended to help students learn the content of English? What content is that? At the very least it's whatever instruction is given in literature, language, and knowledge about writing, and in some cases can include mass media, journalism, and much more. We can hardly be convincing to our colleagues about increasing the amount of writing they demand if we're giving multiple-choice tests on Shakespeare or fill-in-the-blank grammar exercises. How can we urge science teachers to teach vocabulary in context if we still give weekly quizzes from *aardvark* to *zygote*?

The best place to start exploring the possibilities and potential of writing-to-learn is with our departmental colleagues. We can help them rethink what they're doing while they help us. Every English department we've known with more than one member has been staffed with people who disagree with one another. Discussing the possibilities of using writing as a tool for learning in English can provide a positive professional forum for airing and resolving conflicts. The challenges of English teaching are too profound to ignore the best possible way we have of meeting them: using writing to learn.

WRITING TO LEARN

1. Talk to some of your colleagues in other disciplines about the opportunities for writing in their classes. What assignments do they give? How does writing grow out of their classroom activities?
2. Construct a list of the language components in each discipline that's taught in your school. Can you think up some appropriate writing-to-learn tasks for the components?
3. Choose a topic area from within science, mathematics, social studies, or the arts (including literature) which is most relevant to your professional concerns. Make up a learning activity based on the three-stage process described in this chapter, involving some writing which allows your students to explore the topic area.
4. Have the faculty in your school create one writing assignment for each of their disciplines based on the three-step process introduced in this chapter. Duplicate these; you have now begun a writing across the curriculum program in your school.
5. Try out the learning activity devised in Task 3 with your students or do it yourself if you're not teaching.
6. Briefly discuss what learning occurred as a result of the writing completed

for Task 5. How did you or your students react to this assignment?

7. Speculate on some possible ways of evaluating the writing to learn assignments faculty came up with in Task 4.
8. Ask your faculty to evaluate their assignments (Task 4) based on the five-question criteria we've listed in this chapter.

6

Initiating and Sustaining Composing

Jimmy Britton tells a story about a writing class he once observed. The teacher was trying to find a way of motivating her students to do some writing. In the middle of her lecture she hit upon the idea of throwing a lighted match into a paper-filled waste basket. The result: a roaring, smoky fire. Instead of stimulating writing, the fire filled the room with smoke, everyone began to get teary-eyed and started to choke, and all had to leave the room until the smoke disappeared. Britton's moral was clear: we shouldn't depend on artificial stimuli for initiating writing. Not only can they "backfire," but they provide no long-term motivation for writing and very little short-term stimulation either.

We've already quoted Britton as saying that all of life is a preparation for writing, but it bears repeating here. Every child from kindergarten on has had a host of experiences and emotions which can serve as material for writing. It's our task to tap these inner resources and convince our students that such material is a valuable source for writing. We must find ways of getting students to divulge their passions, share their favorite stories, and even occasionally work through their fears and apprehensions. All of these are directly related to their own lives and as such the student writer is the expert on them. Further, they require no outside spark, except a teacher's genuine interest in students and their experiences.

Although these reasons for writing are valuable for all students, they may be most effective for those students who need to feel comfortable with writing. They'll also serve as the basis for the more formal writing that we want to provide for. The question is, when we've succeeded in getting students to write about their own experiences and emotions, how do we keep the energy flowing?

Talking

The best ways to initiate and sustain writing are talking and reading. Genuine talk in the classroom can lead to genuine writing. By "genuine talk," we mean students involved in meaningful discussions with fellow students, teachers, or members of the community who have been invited into the classroom to share their experiences. Through talk, students work out and exchange ideas on a given topic. This doesn't mean that we give students topics, which they then discuss and write about. We can't force topics on students. They must be interested and knowledgeable enough or want to find out more before they're willing to share their ideas with others. They must also believe that there's need for talk and an environment where talk is respected and judgments restrained.

Our first job is to create that kind of environment. Wherever and whenever we can, we must provide opportunities for active and purposeful conversation. Only through encouraging as much talk as possible will students be convinced that talking is a valuable tool for learning and a natural prelude to writing. We must model appropriate responses to talk. We don't want students telling each other they're dumb just because of conflicting points of view. We can show them through our own behavior that disagreeing doesn't mean that one person is right and another wrong, or one stupid and another smart, but that disagreement, compromise and mutual respect for opinions are the hallmarks of useful discussion. If we permit opinions to be ridiculed, we'll be faced with some students never wanting to talk again, at least in a school setting. Without trust, some of them will refuse to participate, especially when they know their opinions or interpretations differ from the group's.

We can encourage genuine discussion by helping students learn what it means to support a position and how to do it. It will also help if we can teach students the benefits of compromise and help them learn when it's necessary. All of these things can be transferred into our students' writing. As we said in Chapter 3, talking about "things" clarifies one's ideas, opinions, and conclusions about those "things." Hearing what others have to say helps us to clarify what we want to say or write, as well as giving us new possibilities we might not otherwise have considered. Talking with someone else provides the best kind of sounding board for our ideas, as long as we're shielded from unnecessary criticism. Having students write immediately after an interesting and lively discussion can be the best way of initiating interesting and lively composing. And sometimes the most effective technique of all is to stop the discussion while it's still rolling along vigorously and have everyone continue it in writing. This can combine the excitement of talk with the wider participation possible in writing.

One example of how talk leads to writing comes from two first grade classrooms in a small town in western Arizona. We were conducting a writing across the curriculum in-service workshop and had suggested to the teachers that before they give students a writing assignment they might talk about the topic to see what ideas the students had, then put some of those ideas on the board, or at least, some of the vocabulary words which might come up;

then allow students to use these "brainstormed" ideas as a basis for their writing.

The teachers protested that if the ideas and vocabulary were on the board then all the students would write about the same things, using the identical vocabulary. We responded: "Well, that's O.K." If there's no basis upon which students can begin to write, they're going to have a very difficult time trying to find ways to get their ideas down.

Later, we observed two first grade classes in the same school dealing with a topic for a PTA writing contest. Unfortunately, the topic, entitled "What Makes a Good Citizen," was one of those artificial ones, but still we discovered a startling difference between the way the two teachers approached the writing with their students.

In one classroom, the teacher put the topic on the board. She instructed the students to print their names in the upper right hand corner and the title two lines below. This took quite a bit of time because the children, first graders, remember, were unsure about her directions and very nervous about putting their titles in the wrong place. In addition, this was to be the final product; they would get no chance to do it over, so it had to be right the first time.

After about 15 minutes all the children had completed putting down their names and the title. They were then instructed to write about the topic. No discussion. The children sat there. Finally, one little girl raised her hand and asked the teacher what a "citizen" was. The teacher defined it and gave an example: "A good citizen is someone who helps other people." The children proceeded to write this down. Everyone wrote the same sentence and each time they came to a word they couldn't spell the teacher spelled it out loud, but didn't write in on the board. After another 15 minutes or so they had added nothing more than that one sentence. Again, they all stopped, looked around at each other, fiddled with their pencils, squirmed in their seats. Not one child had anything else to write about. Then a couple of them started to ask the teacher what else could make a good citizen and the whole process was repeated.

What a painstaking task: the children had no idea what the topic meant, much less what to write about. They were all so anxious about neatness that they kept erasing and rewriting each word over and over again, never getting the chance to experiment with either word choice or sentence structure. It was a frustrating experience for them (and for us).

In the second classroom, we observed a totally different approach. The teacher put the topic on the board, but the students weren't asked to write about it immediately. Instead, she talked with them about it first. She explained what a citizen was, and then she asked them what things they thought might make a good citizen. Linda, in the second row, spoke out, "A good citizen is someone who takes the garbage out every day." Michael, who we had noticed squirming earlier, added, "Someone who helps people cross the street"; and Theresa chimed in, "Someone who salutes the flag." Suddenly everyone was raising hands and giving ideas, and the teacher was putting them on the blackboard. When it looked as if everyone had run out of ideas, the teacher explained about the writing contest and said they were all going to try to write a first draft about "What Makes a Good Citizen."

The children set to work enthusiastically. Their interest had been piqued by the discussion and they were excited about giving examples of what they each did in their own lives that related to being a good citizen. Talk continued as they wrote; as new ideas came up they were shared. Because they knew they would be able to rewrite these papers, they were much less concerned about neatness and misspelled words, although if a new word came up they'd ask for a spelling and the teacher wrote these on the board. But, generally, most of the vocabulary was already up there and they were able to construct their own sentences using these words. Obviously, many of the children included the same ideas about what makes a good citizen, but each of them chose their own individual way of representing those ideas in writing.

What can we learn from these two classrooms? First, talking does not lead to cheating or copying. By having children talk out their ideas and contribute to a class list of possible good citizen attributes, the teacher in the second classroom was actually much more successful in avoiding duplication than was her colleague. Because the children hadn't discussed the topic before writing about it in the first class, they had to rely completely on the teacher, with the result that their papers reflected the teacher's ideas on the topic and her exact words.

This brings up a related point: even though there may have been similar ideas in the second class's papers, what was finally written represented the children's own ideas. They had the oral language capacity to produce words such as "garbage" and "salute," even though they lacked the independent ability to spell and write them. Because these were their own ideas they were much more interested and enthusiastic about writing them down. And since the teacher didn't write out complete sentences on the board, but only vocabulary, the children were actually constructing and writing their own sentences.

Finally, we must view writing as a way of stretching vocabulary, not constricting it. The teacher was building the children's confidence by writing their own words on the board. Obviously, these children had a far more advanced oral language than their written one. But we must be able to show our students that they do possess a lot of language, even if they aren't able to spell it all. How much more confident these first graders must have felt knowing that these were their own ideas in their compositions and that the language was theirs as well.

Just one more point about talking and writing. It seems to us that what happened in this second classroom is an ideal way of developing the kind of workshop atmosphere necessary for writing in school. Through talk the children were able to discover that others in the classroom had different ideas from theirs and that they could help each other through sharing. By building this congenial climate for talk, the teacher was beginning to develop the same qualities which would be necessary when the time came for revising and editing. The children were getting a sense of each other: who they were, and how they could work together to produce better writing, and, of course, more and better ideas. Talk is the foundation, it seems, for everything that comes after it.

Such an atmosphere of trust and collaboration is easier to develop in a self-contained classroom than in a departmentalized secondary school. Students who are together all day identify themselves with Ms. X or Mr. Y and with only minimal encouragement will readily develop a community feeling and, often, a real sense of pride. It's harder to feel that way about 5th period biology or about being one of Ms. Z's second period sophomores. Furthermore, younger children are usually more open to sharing and collaboration than are more jaded and more peer-conscious adolescents.

Even among adolescents, however, a sense of community can be built through talk. This means setting the right tone during the opening days of class. One good technique—ironically, it works best in the relative anonymity of a large school—is to have students divide into pairs with someone they know only slightly or not at all and to interview each other as the basis for a brief written profile. Each writer/interviewer should know that he will have to read the profile to the class to introduce their interviewee to his peers. We find this works best as a low key, unpolished writing task whose first purpose is to produce good feelings and a sense of community. As such, it has the advantage of offering an accessible source of information for the writer and a genuine reason for the class to be the audience. Since the process is reciprocal, each writer has an interest in doing the best job possible. The few hours it takes to interview, write, and share these profiles can be golden for building rapport and community, and perhaps even more important, for providing an engaging first model of the kind of composing that will characterize writing in the class.

Reading

When we have asked teachers to note some of the percolating activities they have used with their students, one of the most common answers has been reading. English teachers in junior and senior high schools have spoken to us about using literature as a source for student writing; elementary school teachers have described how they've read stories and poems to their students who have then gone off to write poems and stories; history teachers use texts, journal articles, newspaper stories to which their students respond in writing; science teachers employ similar reading material for their students' writing. In all, the written material provides ideas, sources, points of view, and sometimes models for students to use in their own writing. Another, less explicit, benefit is that the more reading our students do, the more possible it is for them to develop an "ear" for the written language.

That's a strange analogy, in one sense, since we're talking here about reading, not listening. How *does* reading develop your "ear" for language? We're often confronted with questions about how students learn to write complete sentences; how they learn about organization and coherence; how they learn about introductions and conclusions—especially, how they learn all these things if they're not directly taught. Much of this is learned through talk, but some of the unique characteristics of the written language can only be learned through reading and writing. By providing students with a wide range of reading material—from poems to editorials to technical reports—we're giving them examples of writing that employ the features we wish them to use. The more they read this material, the better they'll become attuned to acceptable standard written English.

A high school English/history teacher related the following revealing story to us. One day she asked her students to read aloud several passages from their history book. She discovered that they weren't reading what was actually on the page; instead, they were reading random words or phrases, often missing the point of the paragraph or an entire section. This revealed to her how their reading process transferred over into their writing; they wrote as they read: random ideas and phrases, resulting in half-articulated expressions of meaning.

One could speculate about a variety of causes for such failures, including the nature of early reading instruction (probably too little focus on meaning; too much on sound/letter correspondence) or simply a lack of reading experience. The major cause of failure to develop an "ear" for the written language may be a failure to recognize that its demands are substantially different from those of the spoken language. One of the functions of using reading in connection with writing instruction is to help growing writers learn to recognize what the demands of the written language are. This is sometimes difficult for young writers. As developing language users, they have had extensive practice with the oral language system and have thereby learned to master the "logic" of conversation. Unfortunately, the "rules" of conversation (like the "rules" of Grammar I, they're followed unconsciously) sometimes give poor guidance to students just learning to write.

There's another side to using reading as a stimulus to writing. The type of reading we've looked at so far is the kind that might be used as source material for written work or as idea-generators for writing. The most recent results of the National Assessment of Educational Progress indicate that students between the ages of 13 and 17 have mastered the ability of retrieving facts from their reading. In other words, they're quite able to tell us *where* Silas buried the money. The real difficulty is in telling us *why*. These results point to one of the most important facets of learning how to read–and one which crosses over into learning how to write–the ability to interpret and synthesize.

We propose that more school time be spent using writing as a response to literature, or to science experiments, or to history texts in which the writing involves students thinking on paper, interpreting meanings, and exploring connections. Instead of asking students to write a critical analysis of the use of Biblical allusions in Blake's poetry, we might ask them to describe what the poem means to them and what effect its words had on their response. These responses could then form the basis of a discussion about imagery. Instead of asking students to answer the questions at the end of the chapter on the American Revolution, we might ask them to speculate on paper about why they might wish to start or suppress a revolution today. As they identify with the feelings that were present in 1776 they might begin to see how history can live today. Before asking students to read the chapter on erosion in anticipation of an essay test, we could have them begin by writing about what they think erosion is doing to the world they live in.

This kind of writing is meant to increase interpretative and sythesizing skills. If we only have them fill in the blanks, or answer the chapter questions, or take the formulaic critical stance toward literature, we continue to deprive them of the ability to discover and interpret for themselves–and future NAEP studes will show even more declines. Speculation, discovery, and interpretation are perfect reasons for self-expressive writing in response to reading. And making personal connections through writing can lead to more technical analyses when and where they become appropriate.

What writers need to embrace and develop is the art of slow reading. In the era of Evelyn Wood there is more pressure for speed reading than for deliberate reading; ironically, slow reading is seen as the problem, not the solution. There are, however, distinctions between types of slow reading. The type caused by a word-by-word or, even more likely, a letter-by-letter or syllable-by-syllable approach to reading is the culprit; the reader moves so slowly that the structures which carry the meaning of the text (phrases, clauses, and sentences) never coalesce. Speed reading instruction, because it increases the size of the text chunks that the reader focuses on to more closely match the meaning-carrying segments, is necessary and appropriate for such readers.

The *art* of slow reading is related to our earlier discussion of developing an "ear" for the written language. It involves reading a text through a second time, either aloud or with full internal resonance as if one were preparing an oral interpretation. The goals are several. First, as noted, to continue to develop an awareness of what the written language "sounds" like, with particular attention to the available options for placing subordinate clauses and other modifiying elements. These need not be labeled, but since appositives, introductory adverbial clauses, nominative absolutes, and the like are more characteristic of the written than the spoken language, a developing writer needs to have some awareness of them before he is likely to be able to use them. While we're not suggesting either direct imitation of, say, E. B. White or Lewis Thomas, or, worse yet, practice exercises on identifying such structures, the slow reading of such exemplary authors will be the best way to develop a feel for these options.

The second thing to be gained from the art of slow reading is an understanding of the power of appropriateness. Every fluent writer has some awareness of word choice both when he is "shaping at the point of utterance" and even more when he is rereading in order to revise. But without the capacity to read slowly, the developing writer will not be able to recognize how each word counts in the final text or to be able to experiment with alternative choices.

Finally, slow reading is essential to the developing writer because it serves as the basis for the scrutiny of one's own text which marks the process of revising. Slow reading will not itself solve the problem of the writer's hearing in his head what he intended to write rather than the words that are actually on the page. Still, with practice such discrepancies will be noticed and adjusted. Thus, slow reading can play a vital part in the revising and editing processes. In attending to others' texts as a commentor/editor, slow reading can pick up nuances and catch errors. Before refocusing on one's own text it's wise to leave it alone for at least 24 hours (that helps to still the false inner voice of the intended text), and then to note carefully where what you wanted to say is obscured rather than clarified by how you said it.

Although we've concentrated in this part of the chapter on talking and reading as the two most important and adaptable ways of initiating and sustaining writing, we don't mean to ignore such things as drama, role-playing, laboratory experiments, observation, filmstrips, and guest speakers. The principles we've used to demonstrate how talking and reading promote and sustain writing can also be applied in as many other ways as teachers will take the time to imagine.

Generating Assignments in Context

This section will show that writing assignments must be sensitive to the development of writing abilities, to the process of writing, and most importantly, to the learning objectives of the teacher and the course content. In Chapter 4 we described the development of writing abilities to be fluency, clarity, and correctness. This development applies to each writing assignment we give. For each new writing task, teacher and student alike will want to pass from fluency to correctness. One consideration about any assignment is what demands it makes on students' thinking abilities. Yet such analysis is difficult because while we may all have a dim sense of Assignment A being harder than Assignment B, most of us would be hard pressed to explain how.

CYNTHIA ONORE I think that an assignment is only good or bad in terms of the context of the classroom, so that it's really important to create an environment of trust between the students and the teacher. Out of that good writing can come. In addition to that, the kinds of writing assignments that I think work best are those that draw on the personal experiences of the students and things that make them think about what they feel about life themselves.

KAREN SHAWN The kinds of assignments that are successful are also those which require some evidence of a need the students have. I started the writing program this year by asking students to write to teachers in the school informing those teachers of the capabilities the students had that were requirements for clubs—for joining clubs—and other activities. It was a real audience, a real need, and the students did remarkably well.

DALE BOYD Assignments will be successful if students know that their writing will be shared with other students in the class, not just the teacher.

Let's say, for example, that a student in social studies is to do a report on "Manifest Destiny and the Rise of American Imperialism." Such a task seems to ask for a generalization-filled exposition written either to the teacher (as tester) or to a mass anonymous audience. Obviously, such an assignment makes quite high-level demands in terms of generalization, type of writing, and type of audience. These levels are probably most appropriate for the upper years of the secondary school, and yet such assignments are quite commonly given in the fifth and sixth grades, which is why youngsters usually copy the paper entirely from published sources, such as encyclopedias.

Another way in which this developmental process could be applied is in relation to the introduction of a new course, or unit. Each new subject we introduce to students presents new challenges. Writing assignments should begin by asking the students to explore, speculate about, or question on paper the new material—writing that is basically personal. Then the assignments should move on toward writing tasks characterized by more focus and organization, and more details, but still asking students to express their newfound knowledge in personal terms. Finally, towards the end of the term, or the unit, writing which demands generalizations about what was learned, or summaries of new information, or conclusions about the implications of the learning to what has been learned before or what might be learned next would be appropriate.

What Would Such Assignments Look Like?

Most of the sample assignments in Chapter 5 spell out what they require, but it's important to remember that more than just the directions themselves must be clear. Both student and teacher should be able to be explicit about the learning objective(s), the procedures to be followed throughout the composing process, and who the audience is. If the writer is unclear about these things, the product may be severely flawed for reasons that have nothing to do with writing ability.

Here's an example of a completely worked-out writing assignment adapted from the work of Laurel Fritz of Tolleson High School:

> *Composing an Owner's Manual*
>
> *Objective:* To better understand and produce a manual for consumer use. Secondary objectives include learning how language can both protect and confuse the consumer and learning how to order and write directions.
>
> *Percolating:* 1. Opening Discussion: "All of us have something we don't like to do (homework? shining the car? washing the dishes?). If you could have a machine which could do this job, what would it look like and how would it operate?" 2. Give each student a blank sheet of paper and have them design their machine. Encourage them to become as detailed as possible.
>
> *Writing:* Students first label the parts of their machines. Then they write an owner/operator's manual describing the use and care of the machine and including such things as warranties, advertisements for it, and instructions.
>
> *Further Percolating:* Teacher and students bring to class as many owner manuals, warranties, and original product advertisements as possible. Students read these, share them, and critique them. Based on these activities, students go back to their manuals and warranties to revise and edit.
>
> *Revising and Editing:* Allow students time to read each other's owner's manuals and make comments and suggestions. After they're satisfied with *what* they've written, have them exchange papers again and edit for punctuation, spelling, etc.
>
> *Publication and Extension Activities:*
>
> 1. Have students build a model of their machines.
> 2. Post illustrations and owner's manuals on the bulletin board.
> 3. Have students construct a booklet with page numbers and an index so each writer can see what his work would look like published.

This assignment has plenty of room for individual students to make it their own, but we suspect that in any class some students would still find this a dummy run. This is probably true of *any* whole-class writing assignment. Which leads to the question of whether or not any assignment can involve everybody. The short answer is probably No. Aside from trying to provide for individual interests and abilities, which this assignment certainly does, the only other solution is to vary whole-class assignments sufficiently so that no student gets bored all the time. The longer answer, however, may require first asking a different question:

How Necessary Are "Assignments" Anyway?

Up to this point we've been making the tacit assumption that most teaching is and ought to be whole-class teaching: teaching in such a way that all the students are doing the same things at the same time. It's a safe assumption that most teaching in American secondary schools is primarily whole-class. Even in the more heavily group-activity oriented elementary grades, what happens more often than not is that each activity group is taught on a whole-class basis, with each group eventually doing what all the others have done. Even most of the "individualized" curricula permit individual differences only of rate of progress; otherwise everyone eventually does most of the same things. Sometimes the more advanced computer-assisted-instruction permits more elaborate diagnosis and prescription matching, but these are limited to very low level skills.

Granted that most teaching is whole-class, the question remains: should it be? The answer is definitely No, at least when we're talking about teaching writing. While some whole-class work is undoubtedly valuable, particularly in those areas of the curriculum with a well worked-out sequence of content and/or skills to be mastered, having thirty children or adolescents writing on the same topic at the same time probably guarantees that some will be bored. It certainly makes sense for all students in a class to be involved in writing at the same time (remembering that writing is being broadly defined and that the composing process includes reading and thinking time as well as pen-to-paper time). It's also probably necessary to have some framework of deadlines to accommodate the inevitable pressures of evaluation. But students should be writing on their own as much as in response to teacher assignments. There are three ways this can happen; two of them seem promising, but the third usually leads nowhere. This is the "free choice" option which teachers either give in addition to or in lieu of an assignment. "Write on anything you want" seems like an ideal assignment for the student; after all it won't be someone else's boring topic. But nothing strikes greater fear into the novice writer than having no guidelines, no direction. Teachers who give it as an option find that students rarely choose it, and even when one or two do, the results aren't encouraging.

What works better than "freedom"? Essentially, freedom in context. Either freedom within the context of a particular assignment or freedom within the context of a writing class with a wide range of individual options. Freedom within a particular assignment is both "given" by the teacher and "seized" or "appropriated" by the student. It's given by the teacher in the sense that Laurel Fritz's assignment asks the students to identify a personal task they dislike and then gives extremely flexible possibilities for designing and describing a machine and owner's manual. And The Declaration of Independence assignment in Chapter 5 gave a wide variety of choices of voice, purpose, and audience. Most good writing assignments contain the possibility of that kind of customizing; indeed, many demand it.

More important than being given options by the teacher is for the student writer to learn how to appropriate assignments. Part of this depends on other considerations such as audience, but part also depends on teachers helping students learn how to make even the most boring topic their own. One of the ironies here is that good students do learn how to do this independently and it pays off in producing strong papers which lead to academic success. Less able or less motivated students either don't see much point to it, or simply don't know how. And we have tended to keep processes like this a secret as though, somehow, it would be cheating to teach pupils how to do things like take tests and appropriate assignments.

How to do it is easily taught and in some ways easily accomplished. What's involved is a game of "let's pretend." The student pretends she cares about the topic and that she's writing to a real audience. This may seem a bit silly, but it's important for every growing writer to recognize that in the real worlds of school and work, there will inevitably be times when like it or not boring writing tasks must be done—taking essay exams, for example.

Why should a student be encouraged to go through such a charade? The shortrun answer is that such approaches make the task more fun and usually result in better grades. The more important longrun answer is that unless one attempts to see new possibilities and ranges of interest, one is doomed to limited horizons. In some cases what seems boring or useless or remote at first acquaintance can become fascinating later on. This won't happen, though, if one's negative judgment is so quick and inflexible as to forbid any shift of focus.

A well-known sentence found in discussions of modern linguistics is: "They are boring students," which is cited for its ambiguity. In one meaning "they" (the teachers) are the villains; in the other, the students are. We would like to suggest a third: they are boring each other. The excitement of learning must be mutually developed and there's as much responsibility on the learners as on the teacher. Learners who can take command of the writing assignments they're given will find that writing is more fun, more successful, and, above all, leads to more learning. Freedom within the context of a writing class with a wide range of individual options is the most desirable way to achieve this state of affairs. In such a workshop atmosphere, everyone is a writer, and when the occasion demands it, a reader-responder or reader-editor. These last two roles will be discussed in more detail in the next chapter; here we'll focus on how a writer finds freedom and support in such an atmosphere.

In this kind of workshop class, writers are free to work on their own projects some of the time, on options for assignments provided by the teacher some of the time, and sometimes in collaboration with others. Within the limits of the grading system, timing can be more flexible so that student writers can move more at a pace dictated by their project rather than be held to an arbitrary set of deadlines. So, too, can be choices of audience or level of difficulty. The only real requirement is that everybody be working on their writing or with someone else on theirs whenever the time is available.

The support in such a context is harder to see, and the apparent lack of system makes the process scary for many teachers and students. For such a process to work, the support must be there in the form of individualized instruction. This requires the teacher's awareness of each student's strengths and weaknesses and a sense of several possible next steps for him to take. It needn't require very much actual "teaching" time in the sense of direct teacher-student interaction; by far the majority of the time is spent writing, reading, revising, or editing, but the conference time that's required should be as helpful and supportive as possible.

This is clearly a less difficult process to set up in a self-contained elementary classroom than in a secondary school where teachers must cope with five or more classes and 150 or more students a day. The pressure of numbers and the limited available time make it difficult to know one's students very well or to be specifically prepared to help them. The advantage of the secondary school is that the students can help each other more, and they can, and must, learn how to help themselves. Learning to take advantage of whatever school situation he finds himself in is each student's responsibility. We as teachers can help, but each of them has to learn that they move on beyond us and eventually beyond the school, and the sooner they learn how to learn, the sooner they'll be prepared to succeed without us.

The Role of Audience in Shaping Writing

KAREN SHAWN If a teacher listens to what's going on she can quite often find the audience built in. In other words, if a student has a complaint, for instance, about something that's going on, perhaps at home, I might suggest that a letter be written instead of talking to the parents. What if they wrote a note and left it on the table? Or, my students are reading William Safire's column. A boy had a very interesting question which was, "Why does the abbreviation Ms. have a period at the end of it, when, in fact, it's not an abbreviation, in the way Mr. is because it's an abbreviation for Mister?" I said I didn't know; why didn't he write? And so he did and every Sunday he reads looking for his answer.

Creating Real Audiences for Writing

Students see us as the evaluators of their writing, but very few see us as concerned and helpful readers. We need to withdraw from the role of sole reader, editor, and evaluator of student's writing, and become advisors, coaches, facilitators. Coaches don't go out on the field at game time—the players are responsible for the play. This is what we must try to get students to understand: that they're responsible for their own writing.

Acting on such responsibility will involve students becoming readers of each other's work. In one sense, by being readers and responders, students are already assuming an audience role. What we're suggesting here is different. In English classes, students are expected to read on their own and to report on their reading. Instead of writing traditional book reports which only the teacher reads (and since students believe teachers have read the book, they tend to do a pretty perfunctory job on these), students might wish to report their reading to their classmates. Recommending books to be read or avoided gets students away from the traditional plot summary report (which is often copied off the dust jacket anyway) and into a much more critical look at books. This not only helps their reading, but it has another meaningful consequence: if someone else reads a book you recommend, you'd better be on target about it. Having this type of real audience places demands on one's writing that wouldn't necessarily be there if you thought the person had already read the book.

A second audience is other students beyond the immediate classroom. School newspapers, special notices, or reports on events or class activities can be distributed throughout the school. Putting student writing on class or school bulletin boards is a good idea, too.

One of the best real audience situations we saw was in England, but we know it happens in the U.S. as well. A high school class had gone to a primary school around the corner. There they talked to the children (one to one) about stories the younger students wished to have written for them. The high schoolers went back to class and wrote the stories, which they then took back to the primary children for reading and response. Having primary grade children as audiences has a delicious advantage: children this age have no qualms about saying, "This is boring," or "I don't like that," or "That's not the story I asked you to write." Reality can be pretty awful, but truthful readers like this make clear to the writer the importance of audience and how it affects one's writing.

There are many other live audiences, both in school and out, for student writing: in school, the principal, the dean, the nurse, the School Board, the PTA, the coaches; in the hometown, the town council, the librarian, the mayor, the luncheonette owner, the bank president, older people of the community who know its history; and, finally, in the world at large, company presidents, a congressman or senator, governmental agencies, even the President. A little imagination and some support for buying stamps is a small price to pay for real audiences. The problem, obviously, is to make sure that the letters are written about real issues.

Two Concluding Problems

Although learning to write well takes a long time and a lot of practice, we argued in Chapter 4 that it can be a natural process: when student writers are grown in an atmosphere in which writing and reading are normal and meaningful activities, they learn to value the written word and to achieve solid competence as writers. The activities and strategies discussed in this chapter have been designed to foster an atmosphere where such student writers can be grown. We have emphasized the positive side of the process, but at least two problems have frequently been cited by teachers moving to implement such programs.

One of these is not so much a problem as an exclusionary tendency. Some teachers and many administrators have argued that these ideas work only with the college-bound, academically able student. Teachers all over the country, however, have found the opposite to be true: the kind of program we are advocating works better with the average or less able student because the more successful ones have adopted the traditional grade-grubbing, teacher-pleasing, grammar-drilling paradigm. It has, after all, been working for them even if it hasn't for their less achievement-oriented peers.

If such a program is started early enough and sustained long enough, it's sufficiently flexible to permit every growing writer to find his own voice and to have a set of positive experiences with writing. There will be individual differences in achievement, but no one need lack confidence. It's our conviction that one of the most important prerequisites to writing success is self-confidence: "Yes, I can write. It isn't always easy, but I know that when I work at it hard enough I can succeed." This is why we stressed fluency as the first developmental step and why this chapter emphasized motivation and purpose as crucial to successful writing assignments.

The next step in the developmental sequence—clarity—is also reflected in the continual concern for audience. And underlying clarity is an even subtler sense of confidence that comes from believing: "Yes, I have something to say. I know I don't always say it clearly the first time, but I know that when I work on it I can make it clear and people will want to read it." This confidence in the worth of one's intentions and the power of one's ability to communicate is crucial to a willingness to put in the time and effort necessary to succeed. We don't mean to suggest that all this will result in some kind of writing wonderland. But we do believe that this kind of program can have dramatic effects on a writer's confidence and competence.

The other implementation problem related to such programs is not unlike that touched on so poignantly in Herbert Kohl's *36 Children* when one of his former students said to him: "Mr. Kohl, one good year is not enough." That's certainly true for this approach, at least true enough so that teachers should make every effort to help their colleagues move in the same direction. Our main reason for doing the original Sunrise Semester course and for writing this book has been to spread these ideas so that more and more children will have more good years.

But while teachers should work with each other and with administrators to make positive changes, for any given group of students those changes may come too late. One thing that can help is for teachers to let students know as much as possible about what's going on. Students should learn something about the nature of and reasons for the educational controversies surrounding the teaching of writing. This need not be done through insults or even *ad hominem* arguments. Students have a right to know why some teachers love to give grammar exercises and you don't, why some teachers return papers bleeding with red pen marks and you don't. Just as this approach supports making the writing process explicit, students can also learn something of the differences between this approach and more traditional ones.

Such a strategy will not insulate the tender writer from the red pen of next year's teacher or from the mindlessness of drills, but it surely will provide some protection. Furthermore, the strategy discussed in this chapter about helping students make assignments their own will provide strength by giving the writer more control over his own destiny. And, the ultimate defense against any potentially hostile writing teacher is to try to figure out what it is they want and give it to them. So part of our process of helping students prepare for such teachers can be hints about how to "read" them and do what they seem to want.

Nowhere is this likely to be more of a problem than in the transition from high school to college. Freshman writing programs have been fueled for so long by the conviction that no one is teaching writing in the "lower" grades that instructors are often unable to look fairmindedly at the writers in their classes. The traditional college freshman writing program frequently stresses form over content and correctness over clarity. They often feature a heavily prescriptive approach based on one sort of handbook or another containing hundreds of pages of *don'ts*. They may value style to the exclusion of anything else including personal voice or commitment.

While it's clear that we often have quite different standards from traditionalists for excellence in written language, the most important differences between us are about means, not ends. Part of the pre-college advisement strategy we need to give our students is confidence that they can use the process means they've developed no matter what kind of paper they're asked to write. If they can learn to figure out what the real demands are of the program, course, or teacher, they can succeed in spite of pedagogy. After all, real writers have been doing it for years.

WRITING TO LEARN

1. Describe how you could use talk in your class in order to facilitate your students' completing a particular writing assignment.
2. With a friend, try having a conversation where you play someone other than yourself. What did you say and do differently? Did your friend identify these changes? What new perspectives did you gain on your own role?
3. Frame a writing assignment for your students based on a reading you've done with your class. How does the assignment relate to and build upon their competence?
4. Brainstorm a list of percolating activities you might use with your class. Try one yourself. What did you do that provided a basis for writing?
5. Jot down a list of important things that have been happening to you recently. Are there any surprises or new connections for you here? Do you see anything worth writing about? Have your students make similar lists.
6. Take a unit from your discipline and develop several writing assignments reflecting fluency, clarity, and correctness.
7. Choose a piece of personal writing or a journal entry from a student or friend and write a comment which will engage the writer in a dialogue about the writing. Try this out with your class. What kinds of responses did they make?
8. Comment on a piece of student personal writing or on a student journal entry by describing what the student has gained insight into and speculating on how you might encourage the student to probe further.
9. Brainstorm a list of real audiences for your students. What kind of writing might be appropriate for these audiences? Have your students make a list as well.

7

Responding and Evaluating

As teachers of writing we inevitably sort and judge student writers. As their writing passes before our eyes we're faced with a number of critical decisions. Our reactions to any given piece of writing are determined by: 1) our expectations before reading the paper; 2) our knowledge of the writer; 3) our interpretation of the paper's ideas; 4) our sensitivity to the paper's formal aspects; and 5) our image of an appropriate "ideal" paper. What we must also keep in mind are the possible effects of our reactions and judgments on the writer and the writing. When we begin to construe our role in the writing process based on how our responses influence change and growth, we'll be better able to monitor our comments and our evaluation of the writer. We'll see that our impressions need only be partially revealed, that we select and filter according to our best sense of what will be most useful to the writer.

Let's look at this issue from the student's point of view. With you for an audience, the writer is receiving *three* messages. The first two reflect a distinction between responding and evaluating, which in some ways parallels the distinction between clarity and correctness. First, the student might well expect a clarity-related response to the question, "How did my paper affect my reader?" Ideally, this response will open up a range of possibilities: "Did she like it? Did she understand it? Were my ideas clear? Did I use proper form? Can I use my reader's responses to improve the paper if I so choose?"

From this perspective the teacher can be seen as just another reader, however privileged, and her responses, which will be nonevaluative because the writing is still a beginning draft, should stimulate strategies for revision. Whatever responses are offered to the student writer, she must assess them in terms of her sense of what is best, however undeveloped this sense may be. Although we're trying to influence the writer's standards for what makes for good writing, we must be sure that the writer gets practice in exercising these standards as they are in the process of being formed. Otherwise we usurp their ownership and force the writer to be dependent upon us and the authority of our standards.

Second, beyond the reader response message the student writer inevitably has been conditioned to expect some evaluative message: "How does my piece stack up against the writing performances of others?" Students may not really want to hear the answer, nor may we always be anxious to give one. But such answers are often required, and how they are framed and delivered goes a long way toward determining the writer's development.

For instance, do our evaluations consider equally the three aspects of writing from fluency to clarity to correctness, or do we base our judgments solely on how well the standards of conventional form have been upheld? Do we emphasize a student's progress against herself, or do we judge performance only against averaged absolutes? And, finally, does our judgment originate arbitrarily with us as omniscient adult reader, or is there a broader base for writing assessment which the student writer can be made aware of and be allowed to participate in?

JOHN MAYHER Part of the assessment issue is to find ways of assessing whether or not students really understand what they're supposed to be learning rather than to be able to regurgitate some pretreated set of words that aren't necessarily theirs.

JAMES BRITTON Yes. It also means seeing the teacher in a role other than that of examiner, in which teachers are using writing to test whether students have learned something, rather than using it as a means of hastening that learning.

JOHN MAYHER We're talking about assessment, in part, in terms of movement or growth from personal writing to the more impersonal and abstract. In fact, one of the ways of assessing writing growth, I suspect, is to look at how that movement happens.

JAMES BRITTON Writing which fulfills the intention of the writer is good writing. Writing that fails to do that is bad writing. Which means that the feedback on a piece of writing in science, for example, needs to be in terms of how well the language captured the truth of the situation; whether the learning process is successful; whether the student has explored to find something or merely flapped around and got nowhere. So the feedback is concerned with the scientific aspects of the writing and it deals with the language itself insofar as that affects the learning. This means you can't really teach that kind of writing in isolation from the study of the lesson. The science teacher in the long run has to become responsible for the development of the kind of writing that achieves that kind of learning.

The trouble with assessment is that it does tend to sweep the

> board and become the only kind of demand, so that everything is written as though it were for an examiner. I feel very ambiguous about assessment. I know it's a necessity, but I don't think it's a joyful necessity. I think it's a painful necessity. We do have to evaluate in the sense that we do have to make a judgment on the student's performance. Other teachers want it; parents want it; employers want it. So it's part of the educational responsibility of the school. My objection comes when that demand spreads across all our teaching. As teachers we ought to know when we're evaluating and when we're teaching, and not let evaluating spread like a stain over everything we do. Giving a verdict on a student's performance is something you need to do, but do it as little as possible.

Unfortunately, the two messages, response and evaluation, conflict. We want to convey to the writer that we're taking seriously the issues she's confronting in her writing; but we also want her to know that there's a real world out there that will continually judge her performance against a variety of formal criteria, some crucial, others not so crucial. Our attempts at resolving this conflict will be fruitless if we continue to ignore the third message the student receives when all of her writing passes before us as audience. This, which is embedded in the hidden curriculum of the schools, can be put simply: the amount of writing completed by a student is directly proportionate to the amount of writing a teacher has the time and inclination to read.

The development of any ability requires a great deal of practice. As writers we need to write frequently if we're to develop the confidence of fluency which will later lead to clarity and correctness. Although schools may emphasize the importance of practice in skills development, they're organized so that each unit of practice (in this instance, a sentence, paragraph or essay) is supposed to be monitored by a teacher. Were a one-on-one tutorial system in operation, the match would be perfect. Then, presumably, everything a student wrote could be read and responded to by a teacher. But this isn't the case.

As secondary teachers, we may be working with as many as 175 students a semester. Consider the time involved in a two-page paper once a week from all 175 students. Read, reread, and responded to with sensitivity, it's not hard to imagine spending in excess of fifteen minutes per paper. Without pause, more than 44 hours might be consumed, and this doesn't account for the inevitable slowing fatigue that sets in during the responding process. And so we cut corners in an attempt to streamline the operation, the first cut involving the volume of writing that we must read. The constraints placed upon us by these numbers are not startling, but have we considered the reality of these ratios from the point of view of the student writers? The student learns that not only is writing invalid if it doesn't pass before the teacher's eyes, but that finally you don't have to write much in school (and thus in life) after all. A developing ability which demands a continuous and rigorous workout gets denied because the production/monitoring ratios fail to match the student's real writing needs.

What can we do and how does this affect our original dilemma concerning the conflict between response and evaluation? When we recognize that our students taken together can produce much more writing than we could ever hope to read and respond to, the scope of our responding/evaluating role becomes contracted and takes on a new character, one of the reasonable sampler. Simultaneously, the student's role as writer is expanded. In the classroom setting, student writers now share in the responsiblity for reading and responding. We're merely sampling what is now a much greater output, and thus the student can exert some control over what's included in the sample and how it's to be treated.

Students will write many partial and complete papers during a marking period and each of these pieces will be kept in their writing folders. Since the teacher is unable to read everything, students are free to select papers they want commentary on. The goal of the writing class is the explicit improvement of both the writing process and its products. Students can ask for *response* on those papers they hope to improve subsequently through revision, as opposed to asking for *evaluation* on those papers which they see as representing their best efforts. Similar strategies can be used by teachers in other content areas.

Now that the teacher's stranglehold on what gets read is broken, she's free to set up procedures to have students write more frequently for a wider range of audiences. The sampling for evaluation that occurs can be a more rational and deliberate process based on joint student-teacher participation. If you want to see how your students perform on specific tasks—first vs. third person narratives, a descriptive paragraph, a journalistic piece, a research report, or a letter to an editor—you can establish the specific categories for the sampling. With the volume of writing greatly increased, students will be free to choose those papers which they feel best represent their abilities in the established categories. This very act of choosing will help students become more consciously responsible for developing a concept of good writing. Meanwhile your response to student writing will be more flexible. In the classroom writing community that you set up, students will be spending part of class time writing. This will allow them to initiate encounters with you, and you can roam freely to encourage, ask questions, resolve disputes, or hold individual conferences. As some pieces of writing go through multiple drafts, you'll be free to intervene before the student comes to closure. And since reading and responding are now to be shared with the student, especially in the form of peer response groups, you begin to function as a model for how writing can be responded to. You're now a participant-leader in the entire writing process.

Responding to Student Texts

A genuine paper, one which succeeds in tapping and revealing real student purposes, will be filled with ideas and issues. If the student had adequately mastered the formal constraints necessary for exploring and developing her concerns, the teacher can then respond directly as another, though more experienced, human being. This response or commentary must be in the form of personalized dialogue. This shouldn't be difficult given reasonably competent student performances, whatever the age level. Such a smooth state of affairs can get quickly unsettled, however, particularly if students write what we've previously labeled "dummy runs." Emphasizing purpose and audience should greatly reduce this kind of writing. Yet, when we see it occurring we need to get students to identify it as such immediately. Then we need spend no further time responding to the piece, for in the new writing class, every minute of time is valuable. Another problem can grow out of papers that are severely flawed mechanically. This will occur if we're working with groups of students who lag seriously behind grade level. Successful handling of such papers will be the mark of the teacher who has resolved the tensions among the competing constituencies she serves.

Let's consider the following paper:

> Hunting is a good sport after being taught of the weapon, first aid and other sorts of good careful hunting. Always don't go trigger happy and don't shoot everything in sight wait until you have a good view of what you are shooting at it could be a person instead of an animal and I don't think you would want to shoot a person when hunting I hope. Most of all make sure you don't clown around when hunting and keep the gun pointing in the air or toward the ground. No I don't think it's wrong to kill an animal unless you're not going to eat it because Lord created everything he put animals on earth for us to eat, but there are some things we don't suppose to eat and it's in the Bible. Many people hunt for the sport not the animal now I think that's wrong I always say if your going to kill something you myswell eat it. Unless your protecting yourself.
>
> Rob

The mechanics of this paper will not do, even for a ninth grader. The form is so flawed that we have real difficulty penetrating the text to get at the student's concerns. Furthermore, the ideas at first seem banal and simplistic. It's not hard to imagine the teacher coming down severely on this paper from any number of angles. But what about the writer and the context of this particular writing act? If we can imagine this piece on hunting playing a central role in the life of its author, how would such knowledge shape our spoken and written responses? How would we deal with the mechanics? Would we be able to recognize the brave effort that "myswell" represents?

The teacher's reflections on these issues serve as a useful starting point:

> The paper was done in response to an assignment from a composition text to write an essay to convince someone of something. Rob had some things to say about hunting and killing animals. This paper was written in the fall and was the first piece of writing I had had from him that was not extremely labored and awkward. He had definitely been writing for an English teacher only. This paper, even though it is rough, was a breakthrough because he was eager to read it to the class, and the class responded with their own enthusiastic opinions. It was a good day for Rob.
>
> When I first read the paper myself, I was faced with some real choices: fix all those run-on sentences, clean up the "we-don't-suppose-to's," make him go back to get his arguments in some kind of logical order, or do as I finally did, i.e., make a few notes on mechanics—three in this case—and respond personally to one of his "you" statements.
>
> When Rob read the paper to the class, he read the full stops at the right places. Teaching him to put periods and capital letters in is not difficult. The "your" for "you are" is also easily taught. There are other grammar III problems with the paper that would be more difficult to teach, but I'm not sure that they are that important for Rob.
>
> The "myswell" at the end of the page is a good example of phonetic spelling and certainly demonstrates the importance of reading for spelling. If Rob had ever read the expression, he would not have had the problem. And since this paper was written in class and there are no cross-outs or other evidence of hesitance, I don't think he struggled over the word.
>
> As for helping Rob move toward mastery of standard written English, I can only do a little at this stage. The full stops, the "your" and the "myswell" are not too difficult to correct. Teaching the logic that could help strengthen this paper is a real challenge—especially to a person of Rob's ability and perception. And frankly, I don't know how to do it. I just keep trying . . . .
>
> But Rob is writing. That is an accomplishment. In a recent paper he wrote, "Sometimes I hate all this journal stuff but I like to read it after its done." It takes a great deal of wisdom to teach and not to inhibit. I don't always succeed.
>
> *Rebecca Brown*

She immediately recognizes the enthusiasm the class felt upon hearing Rob's paper. Real issues and real audiences reign supreme here; the burden of mechanical forms is of secondary importance. Rob's teacher sees that his written text supplies him with enough cues so that he can adequately read it aloud. Realizing that the convention system of writing relates more to the needs of the ear than to the needs of the eye, she sees that she can map future instruction onto Rob's actual oral performance of his papers, thus demystifying the conventions of writing which are obviously such a burden for Rob.

Response, then, has three dimensions. First, it focuses on the immediate meaning-making process that the student is engaging in. The model in this sense is simply human conversation. Someone says something which in turn makes us ask for more information, suggest alternative directions, seek further clarification, or connect our own images and ideas. We do this naturally, and assuming no ulterior motives, our responses are accepted positively in the spirit in which we offer them.

Second, responses should always emphasize the positive. We need to focus on achievement, however little there is; we need to build up, not tear down. There will be those who assert that we should criticize our students and put them in their place by pointing out their many inadequacies. According to this argument students have to learn to face the real world; otherwise we're being dishonest with them. A positive response is not intended to protect the student from harsh realities. They will be his lot soon enough. Instead, it emphasizes that writers work best in relation to readers who care about what they're saying, not in the presence of those who put them down. Now that students will be writing much more, there will be plenty of time to work on the conventions of writing and to challenge students' misguided and unexamined assumptions. But when we do, students will see that they and their texts matter because the response dialogue has been nurtured in a positive environment of caring.

Third, in responding, the teacher must always consider the developmental context of the writer and the evolving dialogues that have been occurring with him. As teacher and student begin sharing common terms and perspectives, a certain shorthand may develop. This will allow both parties to refer quickly to issues raised by previous papers or to the system of conventions being developed during classroom instruction. With experience a teacher is able to judge the appropriateness of her comments; one that may be perfect on one occasion may be totally out of place on another. Part of what makes a teacher successful in this ongoing dialogue is how acutely she senses when a student is vulnerable and when he is susceptible to being pushed and challenged, is ripe for movement and growth.

LEE ODELL We should be cautious about diagnosing and categorizing writers. Teachers and researchers shouldn't try to read too much into a single piece of writing. That is, I don't think we can look at a single instance of student writing and say this kid is egocentric, immature, and bad. People's performance varies a great deal from time to time, from subject to subject, from purpose to purpose, and from audience to audience. Labels have a way of becoming self-fulfilling prophecies.

Another thing I think we ought to be very sensitive to is the fact that what seems egocentric in one context may not seem egocentric in another. A bit of personal narrative, for example, might serve a very useful purpose in one case and serve an audience need. In another case it might indicate that the writer has gotten off the track and started reminiscing in irrelevant ways.

Two additional papers, written by sixth graders, illustrate how a teacher's response can be framed to establish the flow of personal conversation:

By Andy K.

sounds like a good place for a kid to live

In the summer of 1977, when I was in camp, my family was moving. Later on when I got a letter from my family they told me that they were in the new house and unpacking. They also said it was a beautiful neighborhood, a beautiful park, and a lot of kids my age.

When I heard this I was scared for many reasons. I didn't know anybody. I didn't know the new address to the house, so I couldn't write. I didn't want to move away from my old friends, and I loved where I used to live.

During the summer the only thing I was looking forward to do was to see Jordy and David, but otherwise I was scared.

When I got home from camp, I played with Jordy for almost the rest of the summer.

clincher When school started I loved it and now I am glad I moved.

Besides, my best friend Jimmy Lochakanoo hasn't called for three years.

The End

Teacher's Comment:

Andy, I can really hear you speaking when you describe meeting the boys and how you were "looking forward" to these new friends, and yet still remained "scared."

What a CLINCHER you added to your story about moving.

I really see why you love your new house. You really told exactly how you felt.

How do you feel about your home today?

Ping-Pong

By Robert E.

My father, brother and I played ping-pong.

My father and I were about to start the first game when I told him I had to get my sneakers on. Then an idea came to my head.

Now I was in my room. I was going to try to psych him out. He always wears his sweat clothes when he plays me. So, I put on my Fila shirt, a pair of tennis shorts, sweat pants, a tennis hat and a sweatband.

Downstairs now, I walked into the ping-pong room. At that moment my father was beating my brother.

The score was 8-3, with my father winning, when I took off my sweat pants. That psyched him out a little bit, but it didn't help.

After I had lost that game I went upstairs again.

In my brother's room I was looking for a tennis glove. I found it. I also found a knee brace and a sweatband matching my other one. I put them on.

My father and brother finished their game, so I took a paddle. Before the game started I said, "My knee is itching." So, I picked up my sweat pants and scratched my knee brace.

"What's that for?" asked my father.

"To psych you out!" I answered.

We started the game and like ususal my father led through out it. Then he finished me off by a score of 21-15.

My father had played me three times and my brother three times. He won every game by at least three points.

Teacher's Comment:

Bob, between the two brothers can you come up with a strategy to beat your father? Maybe your mother could help? Does he win at other games too? By the way, where did you get the original idea? Another thought—how far has it brought Nastase (spelling)??? Maybe you could write about a few of these ideas in your journal. Have you ever psyched the teacher?

In each instance, the teacher has addressed the student by his first name, which immediately sets the right tone. The opening of each comment lets the student know that the teacher has read and understood his intentions. From there the teacher goes on to raise new questions that might get the writer to elaborate on the topic in ways as yet unconsidered: "Have you ever psyched a teacher?" Being able to risk such a question, the teacher doesn't fear displaying her hesitancy over the spelling of a name. Such a natural gesture should help create an atmosphere of trust in her classroom. Finally, note how the teacher reinforces the use of a technical term, "clincher," that she's introduced during previous class discussions. All in all, the care this teacher has shown here demonstrates to her students that she takes them and their subjects seriously.

Collaborative Response Groups

By setting up peer response groups we begin to share responsibility with our students for the role of audience. These groups must be predicated on three principles: 1) Members must trust each other before committed writing will be shared; 2) Although the purpose for response groups is to help students understand and thus revise and improve their papers, such proposed help can only be acceptable to an author after the need to share and consider the substance of a paper has been satisfied; 3) Students do have responses to the papers written by their peers, but they generally have no developed vocabulary for expressing them. In other words, the elaborated "whys" underlying immediate responses—"I liked that section of the paper," "How could you have written that mess," or "That was great"—need to be developed if group discussion is to help students. It's not difficult to see why peer writing groups don't function smoothly at the drop of a hat, but require patience and persistence on our part if we truly want to integrate them into classroom writing routines.

Building on these three principles, four facets are involved in peer response: *sharing, mirroring, responding, helping.* In *sharing*, students need to get almost pure support for their efforts as writers. They need to see that their writing is really a gift to the group, and that the group welcomes it. In a real sense the first response in these three- to five-member groups is simply silence and pleasure at having taken in the unique expression of another writer; *sharing* is celebration. Our initial urge shouldn't be to criticize or interpret; we should instead revel in such pure acts of communion. Thus, the first week or so of peer response groups may simply consist of each member *sharing* several papers.

Mirroring occurs once it's been established that the writer is liked and accepted as a part of the group. We can like the writer and dislike a particular piece, but student writers have difficulty separating the two. A writer has specific intentions about her writing. Once a piece is finished, she presumably has some idea about how the paper should affect a reader. But most of the time, except occasionally when a teacher comments (which the student may not understand anyway), intentions don't get tested. In other words, we seldom know what is really happening to readers when they read our work. What information actually gets through? What emotions are evoked? *Mirroring* provides the writer with the opportunity to get extended answers to these questions. She can then be in a position to judge the success of her efforts because now a real test of her intentions has occurred.

The procedures for *mirroring* must be set up deliberately. After distributing copies, the student reads her paper to the group once or twice. By reading aloud, often for the first time, the writer begins to discover problem areas in a piece. It's not unusual for a writer to interrupt herself to make a "correction" or to say, "Well, that's still not right." Once this oral reading is completed, each member in turn "reflects" back to the writer a summary of the central ideas in the paper and his perception of the writer's attitude toward them. It's important that all members do this before the writer is allowed to reply. Otherwise, digressions and futile disputes occur. Also, we're trying to encourage active listening (which means you work at hearing and paraphrasing what a person is saying), so the writer must be silent until every group member has had a chance to speak.

In the case of Rob's paper, group members may give him a list of his arguments surrounding the hunting debate with a conclusion that Rob is strongly in favor of hunting if proper guidelines are followed. It's really at this point that the basis for all subsequent learning within the group setting occurs, for now Rob has within his own control the ability to compare peer perception of what he's accomplished with what he intended. To the extent that a writer feels a gap between intention and accomplishment, she will be amenable to subsequent suggestions for revision. If there's no dissonance or if the student fails to recognize or admit it, later "instruction" will be futile.

Suppose that in response to Rob's paper a student mirrors a summary concluding that Rob is really writing a satire against the "gung ho" hunter. What will his reaction be? Somewhat shocked, he might immediately begin arguing his real point. However, with training in how to refrain from assuming an adversarial stance he would go on to get the reader to locate more specifically those lines that led to this interpretation. In the ensuing dialogue, Rob begins to sharpen his understanding of the relationship between rhetoric and a reader's perception. He may, for instance, see that he has many loose connections among his ideas; that he never follows up on how a hunter distinguishes among animals which "we don't supposed to eat." The dialogue might also suggest that Rob's arguments might be more persuasive were he to present some personal episode in which hunting was demonstrated to be a worthwhile sport. Including such experiences would also help him increase his fluency as a writer.

These last remarks anticipate *responding* and *helping*, which should flow directly from our having held our reading/listening mirrors up to a piece of writing. In *responding,* it's time for serious talk about the ideas at hand and how well the rhetorical forms have served to get them across to the readers. In this discussion, members should freely consider the writing's merits and flaws. If writing is supposed to be linked to serious communication, we only verify that this is happening when we engage the writer with our own reactions to the issues she is raising.

If, for example, we disagreed with Rob about hunting, we would give him the reasons for our objections so that he could either modify his position or strengthen it by anticipating and countering his opposition. To the extent that we don't understand what he's getting at, as in his reference to the Bible, we could also insist on more detail and elaboration, thus strengthening the paper's clarity. Or we could talk about other arguments that might more readily convince us that hunting is a great sport. But mostly this dialogue with Rob might stimulate him to speak about his own experiences with hunting; and once finding his voice, he might be able to redouble his efforts on the topic. With this last maneuver, *helping* has appeared on the scene without our knowing it.

As teachers, we shouldn't be surprised that our first reaction to a student paper is to go immediately to helping. Identifying a problem with someone's writing, whether it be punctuation or illogic, misspelling or lack of detail, leads us to offer solutions. Yet by short-circuiting the other aspects of the response process, our suggestions end up falling on deaf ears, their need never having been properly prepared for. Ideally we should withhold help until it's requested, yet the shape that our dialogue takes in mirroring and responding already implies a set of helping directions that the writer can begin putting together in her own words. How much more powerful these words are when the writer finds them coming from her own mouth. We can imagine Rob, for instance, creating some arguments in favor of hunting or beginning to relate his own hunting stories and the group saying, "Well, Rob, just get that down in your paper." Or as he sorts through some of his mechanical difficulties, seeing that they prevent him from reading the paper aloud smoothly, he may be ready for some unobtrusive instruction in writing conventions and alternative combinations of words, which would improve correctness.

Only after matters of substance and rhetorical form have been fully explored should the group help at editing. Rob will need to internalize his own proofreading skills, but as a conclusion to their treatment of his paper, members of the group might offer help with spelling, agreement, sentence form, and punctuation. Such advice should come naturally at this point and be welcomed as Rob sees that his writing has been taken seriously, has had some impact on his readers, and now needs some dressing up if it's to engage yet a larger public audience.

Modeling the Response Group Process for Students

These four facets will naturally interact, especially responding and helping. This general set of procedures will be the best way to restrain destructive criticism, build trust, and establish the foundation of dissonance the writer needs if she's to assimilate future instruction. But assigning students to groups and giving out a set of instructions will hardly guarantee success.

Instead, you'll need to model the process with the entire class. Once your class has been placed in a circle, you might begin your modeling with a student paper from another class. This paper should be no longer than two pages, and though not perfect, it shouldn't be crowded with obvious mechanical difficulties. After you read it several times, ask other students to read it aloud, attempting to get them just to savor what the author has to say.

Next you *mirror* the piece, by giving back in your own words what you heard the author saying and by commenting on its tone or the author's attitude toward the subject. Then ask students to practice mirroring under your guidance. Their tendency will be to take shortcuts like, "Rob's piece was about hunting, and he says it's okay." Such a summary fails to capture any complexities of the author's intentions, and so you must demonstrate and prod them into making more solid summaries such as, "Hunting is a good sport if we don't fool around and if we know what we're shooting at. The hunter should always eat what he's killed, but eating animals is okay because God said it was. Rob obviously thinks hunting is important, but he admits that many people kill animals, but don't eat them, so I'd say he's got a problem here if so many hunters are abusing hunting." Practice at mirroring and your own explanation of how it fits in with the other aspects of the response group process will prepare students to function independently. Once the mirroring format has been settled, your students will be able to monitor themselves, but you can already be encouraging this self-sufficiency in the large group by asking other students to comment on what's wrong when a summary is too clipped or vague.

The difficulty with modeling *responding* isn't in getting students to discuss the ideas; rather, it's in finding adequate ways for integrating talk about form and intention. Let's say, for Rob's paper, that the talk gets around to the issue regarding the animals that God has forbidden us to eat:

1. No I don't think it's wrong to kill an animal
2. unless you're not going to eat it
3. because Lord created everything
4. he put animals on earth for us to eat,
5. but there are some things we don't suppose to eat
6. and it's in the Bible.

In this instance, we need to relate the ideas that are only partially formed in Rob's mind with the structures used to express them. The sequence here begins with "No," which posits an audience out there being addressed, one which somehow has raised the moral issue of killing animals. Rob says that it's not wrong, but the next unit (2) immediately raises some doubts about this killing. This probably causes Rob to sense that he had better strengthen his original position, and so he continues with (3) and (4) where the Lord created animals for our pleasure. Then we get the "but" qualification of (5) before the final authority statement of (6), "and it's in the Bible." Such a conclusion takes him full circle; the Bible is his source for the "Lord created everything," which was meant to justify the hunter killing an animal in the first place.

What's interesting here is that the structure shows Rob torn in two directions. He wants to state flat out that killing animals is okay; but he's really having a pro and con conversation here with himself in which the issue isn't totally resolved. We frequently see this conversational structure embedded in student papers because they're still debating the issues in their own minds. By showing students how their forms reveal this ongoing questioning, we can encourage this very inquiry. This is what we mean by saying that writing can be used to discover—that it functions as a tool for thinking and learning.

The structure of Rob's logic will need to be pointed out to him at some appropriate time, if he's to further his thinking and become more sophisticated about argumentation. He needs to learn that mere appeals to authority will not win the day. Yet given what we know about Rob's development as a writer, a responding discussion of his paper would probably never reach the sentence-level details described above. Such analysis would only undercut the other kind of composing achievement this paper represents. Still, we should not lose sight of how talk must finally integrate issues of form with those of content.

Helping should be modeled with a light touch. Rob's teacher wisely didn't overload him with too many corrections. And, in fact, the first time around, editing corrections should be kept at a minimum, with suggestions for alternative approaches or elaborations emphasized. With the topic "hunting," Rob's intentions have been tapped, so it shouldn't be difficult to encourage him in other attempts at explaining his views.

Modeling these dimensions can't be rushed. At appropriate moments you'll want to make use of an overhead projector to keep all the students attending to the parts of a paper under discussion and to focus on the details of structural reorganization you're illustrating. With practice, your students will be able to work on their own, which will free you for individual conferences.

Once your students are on their own, it's important that you not interfere with a peer group's natural dynamics. You'll have to use your own judgment about grouping students, but once they're chosen, you must preserve the group's integrity so that trust can develop. Only rarely will you need to rearrange a group because of some destructive personality clash. Once the groups are operating, you become the resource writer in the class, the person who can be called upon to mediate disputes or offer advice. Finally, although you'll continually be monitoring the entire group process, you'll find that such monitoring is best done peripherally. Only occasionally will you need to sit in with a group to get them back on track; as their competence grows, they'll instinctively follow the positive tone you've been modeling for them.

In getting students started in the peer response process, it will probably be useful to give them some written directions about their roles. One such set of directions was developed by Lynn Jett of Scottsdale High School, Scottsdale, Arizona:

Directions for Students: Peer *Response* Groups
(not peer attack group, or peer praise group)

Purpose:

To get some reaction to what you have written from another audience.
To see if your writing is clear and easy to understand.
To get help developing ideas.
To get suggestions for improving proofreading.
To get help with spelling, capitalization, grammar, and usage.
To be forced to spend some time writing a rough draft.
To experience the writing process.

Responsibility of Group Members:

1. The group is made up of three people: leader and two responders.
2. The leader is the person whose paper is being read.
3. The leader is responsible for leading the discussion for his/her paper.
4. The responders react to what is written:
   a. they compliment what is good
   b. they make suggestions for improvement
   c. they simply react to the content of the paper
   d. they ask questions about the content of the paper
   e. last and least, they make comments about the grammar, etc.
5. If the leader needs more information or help with the paper, he/she must ask for it.

Toward Healthy Communication in Groups:

1. Speak only for yourself. Say "I." Avoid saying "we," "people," "everyone," etc. Assume that others can do the same. Help each other, gently, to do this.
2. Check with other members of the group when you're not sure what they are saying. Example: "Do you mean . . . ?" "Are you saying . . . ?"
3. Describe the behavior of the other member and how it has affected you. (This tends to show that you are listening and receiving their message.)

4. Try to avoid telling other group members how to be or how to feel.
5. Avoid solving other's problems for them; only *they* can do that. Help them clarify their problems, feelings, issues.
6. Avoid judgment as much as possible: observe and share feelings.
7. Listen very actively: How would it feel for you to be that person presenting that situation?
8. Look at and speak to the person to whom you are giving a message. Be attentive to nonverbal as well as his/her verbal responses.
9. Be brief, be clear, and begin personal sentences with "I." Avoid generalizing. Stay with your feelings.
10. Deal with immediate concerns and the effect they have on you here and now.

TRY TO AVOID BEGINNING ANY OF YOUR SENTENCES WITH "YOU."

WATCH OUT FOR FRAGILE EGOS!!!! Be careful how you make comments. Say what you need to say in a gentle way.

Conferencing

In an eighth grade class in New Jersey recently, Janet wrote the following expressive piece of writing:

He's Gone

I had this horse I called Sunny for 2 months. I got him for my birthday and I was so surprised. We have this big old barn in the back of our yard where we keep him. We get hay for the barn from one of my fathers friends for free and we get the food from our town store for ½ price because I help bring packages out to peoples cars. Were not a real poor family, its just that I have 4 brothers and 2 sisters which all go to private schools which cost alot of money. After I got home from school my father was waiting at the barn door for me, he looked sad. When I got closer to the barn I knowtist Sunny wasn't there. I was just about to run in the barn to look for him when my father said "Sunny had to leave, we couldn't keep up the payments for him." My father explained that my oldest brother was going to go to college next year and we had to save money. Well, that must have been the worst day of my life because something I loved so much had just been taken away. When I turned around my father was gone, so I just leaned against the barn door and remembered the day we got him.

Her teacher's written response spoke to the real issues Janet was engaging in her writing and encouraged her to write further:

> I know that this was a very painful moment for you. Thank you for sharing it. Did you get another kind of pet?

After she got back the paper from her teacher, Janet saw that the teacher's comment was a real one, one which demanded expansion on her part, and so in a follow-up conversation with her teacher, Janet responded accordingly:

J: My father said I could have a dog since they don't cost so much.
T: Yes, I know you could never replace the love you had for Sunny.
J: He was special.
T: Did you get a dog?
J: Yes. His name is King. He's a Labrador Retriever and Wiemaraner mixture. He's really cute and funny.
T: Would you like to write a story about him, tell me all about him?
J: Yes.

Janet went on to write a lively story about King.

In the same class, Stephanie wrote about her experience with Mrs. Winifred:

> I have heard once upon a time of a little old lady who lives on a hill deep in the woods. Some people say that she is lonely but when I met her I knew they were wrong.
>
> The cottage she lives in is nice and neat. The floors are sweeped the table cloth is clean and the windows are crystal clear. In the house she has many friends, as a kitten and a parrot who she talks to all the time. Some people actually believe they talk to her.
>
> Every morning the old woman goes out and feeds the squirrels, the birds and the ducks. She loves the ducks. she never goes a day without feeding them except one day when she was sick. All the ducks came wagleing up to the door squeeling and squalking. When she came to the door the ducks were standing still squeeling and squalking, she took some bread from the cupboard and fed them.
>
> Then one day a man from Littleville City drove down to the little old woman's house.
>
> He knocked on the door very hard and had a stern face. when she answered the door he barged in without invitation. Mrs. Winifred, I'm from the city department and we would like you to move, we think we found oil around here and there is gonna be drilling. You have to be out by next week.
>
> When the stern faced man left, the old woman went to feed the ducks for the last time.

With great sensitivity, the teacher describes the importance of this piece for Stephanie and what their subsequent conference accomplished.

> When talking with Stephanie about her story, I discovered that the little old lady is her great grandmother who lives in another state and who was actually forced from her home because of a large industrial complex. This is the best writing Stephanie has done, and the subject is obviously one which touches her deeply. I'm sure that this is a factor in her improved writing.
>
> I have encouraged her to see if she can find out if such things ever happen in our state. I suggested that she inquire about the treatment of Senior Citizens in our town. She will find out that there are special accommodations for them and that we have agencies which step in to help them.
>
> This will not only give her an opportunity for more writing but may help her deal with her feelings about her great grandmother. She's in the process of doing her research now and says she'll write all about it.

Stephanie later wrote about her great grandmother and attempted a report on the lives of the elderly in her New Jersey town. With these two young writers, the teacher knew that conferencing was a way of stirring up more writing while legitimizing the writing already completed.

Conferences will be as various as the number of writers in a class, but they should be conducted in light of what is most pressing for the writer at the moment. The trick is finding out what items the writer wants placed on the conference agenda. In the examples above, the teacher saw through to the issues that concerned these girls, but often we may not know what is on the writer's mind. What better way than to ask directly, "What in particular would you like us to talk about?" or "What shall we accomplish in today's conference?" In a rich classroom writing environment, we'll be surprised at the range of answers. Initially, students need to build confidence in us, to hear positive and supportive remarks. Second, they need feedback to see if they've been understood. Third, by talking about ideas and images, they'll get confirming and conflicting evidence and opinions. And finally, they need suggestions for further expansion or help on various structural difficulties.

Naturally enough, conferences will include much overlap. *Helping*, for instance, may involve not just the improvement of a particular paper, but encouraging the student to explore related experiences through writing. Such exploration will only grow out of good *responding* talk. Thus, Janet's teacher in her brief comment ("I know that this was a very painful moment for you. Thank you for sharing it. Did you get another kind of pet?") is making Janet feel important by focusing on *sharing*, and by referring to the "pain," *mirroring*—letting Janet know that her attitude has been accurately perceived.

The teacher's comment also involves *responding,* by wanting to know what happened next, and *helping,* by opening up a connected topic on which Janet can continue to write.

Janet's teacher ignored the several correctness problems in the paper. There'll be time enough to get the apostrophes straight or learn the difference between *which* and *who.* Should Janet's expressive piece be developed further for class publication, editing groups or editing stations can take over. Also in the natural flow of conversation during subsequent conferences, the teacher might bring up mechanical or formal issues, especially if a pattern recurs. But by this time, Janet may even be initiating the call for instruction herself as she does more reading and actively participates in her peer response group.

Although sometimes the teacher will write comments directly on the student's paper, this isn't necessary all the time. It may prove to be a terribly inefficient use of time now that we're committed to increasing exponentially student writing time. Preliminary research shows that five minutes of intense talk with a student can equal up to twenty-five minutes spent on written comments, and that the talk tends to make a more lasting impression. When the teacher's message is delivered through conversation, the student isn't left with a paper covered with someone else's scribblings.

To streamline conference procedures, one teacher we know in Pennsylvania sets up a triad at her desk. At the beginning of a class period that will be devoted to conferences, the teacher generates two equal columns of student names on the blackboard, one to her left, one to her right. Each list relates to the corresponding chair on either side of her desk. All this happens with a minimum of fuss, and immediately the two chairs are filled by students ready for conferencing, while the other students are working in groups or on their own writing. After she's finished with one student, she turns to the other, who's all ready to begin. Upon leaving, the first student erases her name, indicating that her chair is now free for the next student. In one class period this teacher can speak in detail with about ten students, so every student receives some personal talk from her on writing at least once every two weeks. This teacher doesn't feel that an inordinate amount of class time is spent conferencing; the figures work out to less than twenty percent. Yet her students know that they'll be talking with her on a regular basis, which is her way of showing her concern for their development as writers.

Editing in Its Proper Time and Place

When a teacher notices errors in a paper, she must be selective in deciding which ones to bring to the student's attention. Overloading a student with corrections serves no real purpose except to undermine her confidence as a writer; rather, the teacher should pick out a subset of error patterns that might be worked on. These patterns should always relate back to a concern for clarity and the need to read the paper aloud.

As the teacher recognizes that a particular convention is causing problems in a number of student papers, she might interrupt the class to give a quick lesson on the point. Such teaching at the moment of need can also be blended into curriculum planning in the form of pre-teaching when a new writing task is about to be undertaken. Let's say some younger students are about to tackle dialogue writing. The teacher can unobtrusively point out the use of quotation marks, referring back to instances where the students have encountered them in their own reading. With such an approach, the teacher is attempting to get students to internalize the process of editing rather than keeping them dependent on the teacher. In such an environment the teacher mediates standards, but she shouldn't be afraid to reveal her own vulnerabilities as a writer. If, for instance, she has a problem with spelling, it's better to admit it. This will show students that teachers are human after all.

To get students to internalize the proofreading process requires constant effort. This effort will be best expended in an atmosphere of "publication" in which students begin to comprehend the formal expectations that readers bring to a written text once it has entered the public realm. The majority of student's personal pieces will never be considered from a correction perspective, but once a piece begins to get revised for a more public audience, matters of form can be confronted. At this point arrangements that encourage students to help each other can enforce the idea that you want students to eventually become their own proofreaders.

To begin with, you'll want to demonstrate for your students the value of reading a paper aloud to pick up transcription errors and get a sense of its rhythms. You'll also want to show them how setting a piece aside for awhile makes it possible for the writer to see more readily any problems. Then a number of options are possible. You might have students form an editing buddy system for those papers which are eventually to be evaluated. Or you might form editing groups which take responsibility for proofreading the papers of each of its members. These groups in turn might become specialized, with each forming a specific editing station in the classroom. At appropriate times a student could bring her paper from group to group, getting checked off for spelling here, punctuation there. Experts in each area of proofreading will emerge, and this role gets serious when editors must certify over their own names that a paper has passed muster.

In the near future, computer word processing programs might further support classroom editing. A student could, for example, get a read-out of all the misspelled words in her text. Then she would need to make the corrections herself. In such a case the computer wouldn't be doing the actual spelling work for the students, but comparing words as they're typed in the text with words as they appear in a predetermined dictionary list. Proper names and other words that are spelled incorrectly would get "captured" by the computer's printout, and the student would still be actively involved in the decision-making process with respect to correction.

If we make sure that students are actively involved in the proofreading process at the appropriate time, their anxiety over form will greatly diminish. By avoiding a correction fetish, we lend credibility to our question and advice for the student who brings us a paper for response: "Who else will be reading this paper . . . ? Well, you'll probably want to go over it carefully at least one more time." In such situations the student will know she's not alone, but has the resources of the entire class behind her.

From Assessments to Revealed Judgments: Moving Toward Consensus

As we read student papers, we must keep trying to integrate three variables: 1) our sense of where an ideal student should be at this stage in her development; 2) our sense of where this particular student has come from; and 3) our sense of where we feel this student might move from here. Our assessment of a student's progress in writing could therefore lie along either of two competing continuums: the student's performance judged against itself and the student's performance judged against others. Inevitably the two will be in conflict. Will we want to respond to a student's writing on its merits and as an example of her growth as a writer? Or will we also feel a responsibility to the student to give her a message about how the world will probably evaluate her writing? These tensions are further muddled when the teacher suspends the determining relationship between an assignment and a given product in order to encourage risk-taking and thus leave room for surprises and unexpected inventions on the writer's part.

There are several ways out of this dilemma. First, with the volume of writing greatly increased, students will have more opportunities to succeed and thus the incidence of negative judgments will be greatly reduced. Also, the range of writing tasks will be more catholic so students should find at least some areas where they can feel good about themselves as writers. Second, because we're no longer exclusive monitors of the writing process, we pass on to students part of the responsibility for owning up to where they stand as writers both against themselves and against the wider, more publicly revealed standards of the classroom and the world at large.

Specific ground rules will help enforce the validity of your judgments. Students should understand, for instance, that their personal writing will be assessed only as it relates to their actual learning and will never receive a grade as such. The teacher will grade only revised pieces. Thus, not every teacher reading results in a final judgment. The increased volume of writing, along with the sampling procedure for evaluation, will mean that students must keep *all* their writing. This will pose no real logistical problem and should reinforce the student's sense of growing competence because she'll be able to see and review her accomplishments at regular intervals.

For evaluation, the student chooses work that best represents her abilities. In doing so she might consult other students, thus increasing collaboration among writers. The process of selecting papers for final evaluation and checking them carefully one more time also helps students refine their standards for good writing.

Now that you have a stack of papers for judging, students need to be shown that final evaluations aren't based on arbitrary standards. To do this, you'll first make explicit the criteria you'll use for marking. These will include standards for originality, evidence, organization and mechanics. Again, you'll want students to participate in this process so that they'll understand the rationale behind the evaluating.

Next, you might consider creating a more public forum for judging papers by swapping sets of papers with at least one other teacher. In such a system each student paper would be graded at least twice. Probably you would want to score the papers holistically, with any disagreements arbitrated at the end. Holistic scoring is a straightforward method for sorting papers according to level of achievement. After four to six levels of writing competence are established and representative papers presented to characterize each level, a stack of papers is read quickly by each grader who assigns it a competence-level score. Final evaluation is then based on the average of these rankings. Although this may sound like a complicated and time-consuming procedure, it shouldn't prove overly burdensome; only a quick evaluation is called for, not a carefully considered and sometimes lengthy written response.(For more guidance here, see Myers, 1980.)

Joint teacher assessment helps bring in a touch of the real world because now your students' work is being submitted to outside audiences. Such assessment also helps you share your grading criteria with your colleagues, so that each may learn and adjust accordingly. Finally, in those instances where you're working on student writing with you colleagues in other disciplines, you'll want to encourage them to comment on the substance of the material while you pay closer attention to how it has been presented.

Approaching evaluation in this public manner cleanly divides it from response. No response comments of the kind we've been talking about should be expected by our students inasmuch as they'll have received them earlier. Instead, a grade is recorded along with a brief note relating the grade to the criteria for assessment. Upon receiving this evaluation, students will be free to follow up on disagreements at subsequent writing conferences. By making this division between response and evaluation clear to our students as expressed in our arrangement of instructional patterns in writing, we encourage greater efforts on their part because we've demonstrated to them conclusively that we take them seriously as writers.

WRITING TO LEARN

1. Choose a series of compositions you have commented on and/or evaluated. What's the purpose behind each comment? How helpful were your comments to students? Did they encourage revision? Or demand it? How much attention did you pay to content? to form? How do you know how students respond to your comments?
2. Give your series of compositions to other teachers for comment. How did they attack the problem? What are their answers to the questions above? How do you account for the differences in approaches?
3. Select a set of five papers from one of your classes. What grades would you give them? What would be your basis? Give the same set of papers to several colleagues and have them assign grades. Discuss the differences and/or similarities. How do you go about reaching a consensus?

8

Surviving Together in the Real World

It's Dangerous Out There, So Let's Be Careful

Item: In one high school where some of the English teachers were interested in beginning a writing across the curriculum program, the principal initially gave his support. He didn't really understand the program, however, and when opposition presented itself, primarily from the coaches and the shop teachers, he did a flip-flop; claimed he had never liked the program much to begin with; bad-mouthed the teachers who were trying to start it; and withdrew all further administrative support.

Item: In a K-8 school the principal decided that a writing across the curriculum program would be just the thing for her faculty to engage in. She contacted a team of consultants and arranged to have them spend two days with the staff. She neglected, however, to inform the staff of what was going on, and as a result, the consultants had to spend most of their time dealing with the staff's hostility toward the principal, rather than talking about writing across the curriculum.

Item: A local newspaper printed the various test score results of neighboring school districts on the state-mandated standardized reading, language, and math tests. In one local high school where a writing across the curriculum program had already begun, the principal, under pressure from his superintendent, decided that his survival depended upon a quick-fix of the test scores. He ordered grammar instruction to replace writing across the curriculum. Even though the test scores were originally very high, pressure to make them still higher effectively sabotaged the program.

Item: Teachers of other disciplines involved in talk and planning for a writing across the curriculum program at an urban high school resisted any change in their current approaches. Some complained that asking students to write would require too much reading on their part. Another group had already run off their dittos for the entire year and didn't want to upset their schedules. A third group was concerned that if they had their kids write they wouldn't be able to "cover" all the material in the curriculum. Once again, the department chairs and the principal caved in and the program died.

Item: The English department of another school was badly divided over the issue of how much grammar must be taught. Those teachers who held that knowledge of grammar was a necessary prerequisite to any writing instruction won the day and as a result very little writing instruction goes on at all.

Item: In an elementary school the teachers were convinced that their beginning writers should be doing a lot of writing practice in order to develop fluency. Because they wanted to make the children feel good about what they were doing, some papers were sent home with only positive comments and no effort was made to correct errors. When the parents complained that teachers were not doing their jobs, the principal and the staff panicked and returned to the red pencil for all papers that were sent home.

United We Stand

Item: Two English teachers and a science teacher in a high school managed to convince their superintendent that a writing across the curriculum program would be in the best interest of all the students in the school. Working together with him, the school board, and the principal, the three teachers designed an in-service program which offered concrete practical suggestions and a theoretical rationale for using writing as a tool for learning in all subjects. Although opposition developed from some faculty members, others became convinced that their students would learn more if they wrote more. The continuing support of a well-informed administration and the collaborative spirit of the core faculty have enabled the program to grow and flourish into its third year.

Item: An elementary principal with a large non-English speaking student body became convinced that for students to learn English they must write it everyday in meaningful ways. Through a combination of staff development meetings, the provision of opportunities for publication of student work, and the use of whatever outside help he could get, the school is achieving outstanding results and word of its success is spreading.

Item: After attending a summer institute sponsored by the National Writing Project, the new English Department Chair of a high school and several of her English department colleagues decided to try to implement a writing across the curriculum program. They first informed the principal in detail and secured his enthusiastic support. They next surveyed the faculty about how much and what kind of writing was actually going on in their classrooms. Then they brought in outside consultants to speak to the entire faculty, and set up a successful in-service course for district credit to provide practical advice and further understanding of the processes of writing to learn. The program is gradually being adopted on a teacher-by-teacher basis.

Item: In a junior high school the English department had been trying without much success to interest their colleagues in using more writing. Their efforts had served, however, to prepare the groundwork for an in-service day workshop run by outside consultants on writing across the curriculum. The consultants and the department met to plan the workshop and to discuss the school's specific needs. The workshop was sufficiently successful that many of the teachers were willing to try some of the ideas, and one social studies teacher became such an enthusiastic convert to the idea that she spent the next school year buttonholing her colleagues and encouraging them to try it because "it really works."

Item: An elementary school district curriculum committee in designing a new approach to writing for the district anticipated the need to inform parents about some of the changes which would be occurring. One of their concerns was possible parental backlash about not marking every error in students' papers. They prepared a sample letter which teachers could adapt to send home to parents to inform them about what they were doing and why.

Delayed Gratification

Every school will have idiosyncratic difficulties trying to change. The anecdotes cited above are intended both to caution and encourage. The key factor in a successful effort to bring about positive change is the necessity of working together. While this collaboration can start with like-minded colleagues, it must eventually involve administrators, parents, and the school board as well, or no lasting change will happen. Insofar as these ideas are new ones, education is clearly required. We cannot assume that everyone understands the role of writing as a tool for learning or the requirements necessary for implementing such a program, especially since it flies in the face of the conventional wisdom of their previous experience. Neither can we assume that a process approach to writing, like the one described in this book, is widely accepted or even understood.

As we move to think about the changes that we're trying to bring about, and about our relationships with our colleagues in doing so, it may be helpful to consider the multiple roles we play as teachers of writing. Only by recognizing this diversity can we begin to appreciate the complexity of our responsibilities and the difficulties involved in working with others to get them to change their attitudes and behaviors in some or all of these roles.

1. WRITERS: We need to remember that we're continually modeling the composing process by how we present ourselves as writers to our students.
2. CONVENERS: We're the ones who bring students together in the classroom and create a classroom environment through which we set the standards for how our students will value writing.
3. STIMULATORS: We help students discover reasons to write and people to write to.
4. RESPONDERS: How we read and enter into dialogue with our students

on their papers goes a long way toward shaping their attitudes toward writing.

5. INTERVENERS: We need to choose our moments wisely; commenting and conferencing will encourage and build the writing abilities of our students.
6. INTEGRATORS: We build our students' writing program on the basis of their oral skills and supplement it with extensive reading.
7. MEDIATORS: We must be sure that students understand the reasons for the conventions of writing and that they not become dependent upon us to perform the proofreading function.
8. JUDGERS: We must be sure to separate response from evaluation, making our grading criteria as explicit as possible, building students into the process of establishing these criteria, and creating public assessment procedures.
9. SORTERS: We must remember that not all written work must pass through our hands, and that how we judge a student as a writer can go a long way toward locking him into a set image of himself as a writer.
10. PROSELYTIZERS We're the key advocates for a sane and rich writing program in the schools who must educate and build bridges with colleagues, administrators, and parents if the students' interests are to be best served.

We can't shy away from confronting our colleagues and supervisors just because it's going to be difficult. It will take time to accomplish meaningful change, and there will be moments when it will seem easier to abandon the effort than to persevere. We can plan a gradual approach which allows sufficient time to work through the initial problems of resistance and inertia. Enlisting one or two colleagues per year out of content area departments sounds like a disappointing rate of change. But if progress is steady, the eventual shift can become a geometric progression as the new advocates spread the word.

Those who have been teaching for any length of time are familiar with the waves of curricular and methodological "innovation" which have swept in and out during the past decade or two. Team teaching, flexible scheduling, open classrooms, phonics, new basals, new math, new chemistry and so on have washed over American schools, leaving only the smallest traces of academic flotsam and jetsam behind. One of the reasons they didn't have much permanent effect was that they were usually imposed from without and attached piecemeal to an already overstuffed curriculum. Our goal in recommending the approaches suggested here is to bring about evolutionary rather than revolutionary change. To accomplish this there must be full understanding by all parties of the underlying reasons why this approach can make a genuine difference in student thinking and learning.

The pressure for the quick-fix is particularly intense in a time when schools are under attack and when generally inadequate and inappropriate evaluation measures are being used to hold schools accountable for student learning. Teachers and administrators must become actively involved with their communities in redefining the ends of education and in criticizing simplistic assessments of success. The school boards and legislators who have mandated various accountability measures aren't really aiming to promote superficial learning and a trivial curriculum. They must be shown by school professionals that such well-intended efforts to improve the quality of education often have the opposite effect. In Arizona, for example, alumni of the two National Writing Projects have been lobbying the state legislature and the State Department of Education to change the testing system by showing them the counterproductive effects of the mandated statewide testing program. Schools should welcome community pressure to improve the quality of education, but as professionals we have a responsibility to ensure that such pressures lead to constructive change.

Coming Together

As students move from elementary school to junior high, or from 10th grade to 11th, they have the right to expect reasonable consistency of approach in how they're learning to write and how they're using writing to learn. Although individual teachers will inevitably have some differences of focus and emphasis, shifting from a teacher who has adopted the general developmental sequence suggested here—from fluency, to clarity, to correctness—to one whose priorities are exactly the reverse can shake a student's faith in education and produce academic schizophrenia. If students and parents are to maintain, and in some cases, to regain, their faith in the professional competence of schools, they must have a sense that we know what we're doing and that we broadly agree about both the ends and means of education.

Consistency is important because students develop strong expectations about the way school is supposed to work. By the time they get to secondary school, most students have come to believe that English equals grammar drills and vocabulary tests. The 10th grade students who asked their teacher in March, after a semester and a half of discussing literature and of writing papers they enjoyed, "Now Mr. M., we're having a good time in your class, but when are we going to get to English?" were only responding to their previous experience with a drills and skills based curriculum. Their fear that they were missing something was very real. We must be prepared to make our reasons for a different approach clear, and we must allow students to participate in building the evaluation standards which will let them see how they're growing as readers and writers.

Many teachers and parents talk these days as though students were substantially different in some earlier era. Students today are said to be both less motivated and less skilled as writers and readers and, generally, as learners. Without debating whether or not there ever was a golden age of "studentdom," we're convinced that students can get better as learners and as language users. The whole thrust of this book has been to show how this can be done. Achieving such an end will demand more effort from students, but we believe that the approaches suggested here will make that effort seem worthwhile and result in greater achievement.

It will also demand more effort from the faculty. Most teachers are overburdened and often discouraged. Those teachers who are convinced either that their approach is flawless or that no improvement is possible aren't the ones to start with. Every school we're familiar with has at least a few teachers who aren't happy with what they're doing and are open to the possibility that another approach might work better. If the initial approach is a low-key gathering together of positive-spirited teachers, perhaps as a curriculum committee selected on the basis of their answers to a writing survey, successes can be shared and problems solved.

Small, professional support groups aren't part of the normal daily experience of teachers. Building a system for change will require them. In addition to helping implement a program like writing across the curriculum, such mutual support provides teachers with the resources to overcome those who *know* it can't work. Teachers who participate in such groups look forward to coming to school secure in the knowledge that however difficult the day may be, there are people to turn to for meaningful help.

But administrators must be educated about the whys and hows of such a program. Most principals we know are vaguely in favor of the idea that children should write more and better, but they don't have much of an idea about what role writing can play in learning, or about the process approach to writing. The only way they'll be able to resist the inevitable pressures of cynical faculty members or uninformed parents will be if they have been educated in depth about why this kind of approach is an essential ingredient in developing the kind of quality education that they profess to want. If the curriculum cell and the administration are working together, they can anticipate and prepare for whatever problems may arise.

Another related strategy in trying to implement these changes might be to create some faculty writing groups of the sorts suggested here for use in classes and, if possible, to include administrators as well. Part of the reason it's hard for teachers and principals to recognize the worth of peer response groups is that in their own education they've never had much experience with this mode of learning. It's also the case that teachers, even or possibly especially English teachers and administrators, are just as fearful of writing as the rest of the population. All of us have suffered from a "correctness-first" approach, with the result that writing is avoided where possible and anxiety-provoking when it can't be avoided. Furthermore, teachers working together in a writing group can get practical firsthand experience with the processes of response and revision. They can recognize what a writer really wants and needs in terms of audience feedback and can use these insights as guides to their own teaching.

The approaches we've suggested here do change the look and feel of the classroom and some aspects of the teacher's role. The fear of losing authority is aggravated by teacher fears of excessive noise, unregimented classrooms, student control and so on. No longer is the teacher the only source of response to student work. Students own more of the writing process and its products. Yet, the genuine authority of teachers doesn't depend upon being the constant center of attention. The necessary authority of the teacher depends upon his capacity to encourage student learning. Students may fear the kind of teacher we're advocating here less, but they'll respect him more. We're certainly not encouraging a classroom of chaos and confusion where anything goes. We're saying instead that the teacher who can help a student become the center of his own learning will earn and deserve the authority of a professional adult.

We're not so naive as to believe that teachers' lounges will become, overnight, places where the kids are mentioned positively and where teachers share ideas and practices in a spirit of professional collegiality. But things will not ever get better if we accept the status quo and continue to let the cynics and the nay-sayers dominate our professional lives.

References

Applebee, A. N. *Writing in the Secondary School: English and the Content Areas.* Urbana, IL: NCTE, 1981.

Britton, J. N. *Language and Learning.* London: Penguin Books, 1970.

Chomsky, C. "Reading, Writing and Phonology," *Harvard Educational Review,* 1970, 40, pp. 287-309.

Chomsky, N. "A Review of B. F. Skinner's *Verbal Behavior,*" *Language,* 1959, Vol. 35, pp. 26-58.

Cooper, C. R. and L. Odell, eds. *Evaluating Writing: Describing, Measuring, Judging.* Urbana, IL: NCTE, 1977.

DES. *A Language for Life* (Bullock Report). London: Her Majesty's Stationery Office, 1975.

Dyson, A. H. "The Role of Oral Language in Early Writing Processes," *Research in the Teaching of English*, Feb. 1983, 17, pp. 1-50.

Emig, J. *The Composing Processes of Twelfth Graders.* Research Report # 13. Urbana, IL: NCTE, 1969-1971.

Fillion, B. "Language Across the Curriculum: Examining the Place of Language in Our Schools," *McGill Journal of Education,* XIV, (Winter, 1979), pp. 47-60.

Flower, L. "Writer Based Prose: A Cognitive Basis for Problems in Writing," *College English*, Sept. 1979, 41, pp. 19-37.

Fulwiler, T. "Journals Across the Disciplines," *English Journal*, Dec. 1980, 69.

Goodman, K. S. *The Psycholinguistic Nature of the Reading Process*, Detroit: Wayne State University Press, 1968.

Graves, D. H. "An Examination of the Writing Processes of Seven Year Old Children," *Research in the Teaching of English*, 1975, 9, pp. 227-241.

Hairston, M. "The Winds of Change: Thomas Kuhn and the Revolution in the Teaching of Writing," *College Composition and Communication,* Feb. 1982, 33, pp. 76-88.

Kirby, D. and T. Liner. *Inside Out: Developmental Strategies for Teaching Writing.* Montclair, NJ: Boynton/Cook, 1981.

Loban, W. *Language Development: Kindergarten Through Grade Twelve.* Urbana, IL: NCTE, 1976.

Martin, N., P. D'Arcy, B. Newton, and R. Parker. *Writing and Learning Across the Curriculum, 11-16.* London: Ward Lock Educational for the Schools Council, 1976.

Myers, M. *Procedure for Writing Assessment and Holistic Scoring.* Urbana, IL: NCTE, 1980.

Moffett, J. *Active Voice: A Writing Program Across the Curriculum.* Montclair, NJ: Boynton/Cook, 1981.

Murray, D. M. "Internal Revision: A Process of Discovery," in C. R. Cooper and L. Odell, eds., *Research on Composing,* Urbana, IL: NCTE, 1978.

Perl S. "Five Writers Writing: Case Studies of the Composing Processes of Unskilled College Writers." Unpublished doctoral dissertation, New York University, 1978.

———. "The Composing Processes of Unskilled College Writers," *Research in the Teaching of English*, 1979, 13:4, pp. 317-336.

Rosenblatt, L. M. *Literature as Exploration.* New York: Noble and Noble, 1938/1968.

———. *The Reader, The Text, The Poem: The Transactional Theory of the Literary Work.* Carbondale, IL: Southern Illinois University Press, 1978.

Shaughnessy, M. *Errors and Expectations.* New York: Oxford University Press, 1977.

Scardamalia, M., C. Bereiter, and B. Fillion. *Writing for Results: A Sourcebook of Consequential Composing Activities.* LaSalle, IL: Open Court Publishing Co., 1981.

Smith, F. *Psycholinguistics and Reading.* New York: Holt, Rinehart and Winston, 1973.